THE PSALMS

The Psalms

An Introduction

José Enrique Aguilar Chiu

Paulist Press
New York / Mahwah, NJ

Unless otherwise indicated, the Scripture quotations contained herein are from the New Revised Standard Version: Catholic Edition, Copyright © 1989 and 1993, by the Division of Christian Education of the National Council of the Churches of Christ in the United States of America. Used by permission. All rights reserved.

Cover image courtesy of Zvonimir Atletic / Shutterstock.com
Cover design by Sharyn Banks
Book design by Lynn Else

Copyright © 2014 by José Enrique Aguilar Chiu

All rights reserved. No part of this publication may be reproduced, stored in a retrieval system, or transmitted in any form or by any means, electronic, mechanical, photocopying, recording, scanning, or otherwise, except as permitted under Section 107 or 108 of the 1976 United States Copyright Act, without the prior written permission of the Publisher. Requests to the Publisher for permission should be addressed to the Permissions Department, Paulist Press, 997 Macarthur Boulevard, Mahwah, NJ 07430, (201) 825-7300, fax (201) 825-8345, or online at www.paulistpress.com.

Library of Congress Cataloging-in-Publication Data
Aguilar Chiu, José Enrique.
   The Psalms : an introduction / José Enrique Aguilar Chiu.
     pages cm
   Includes bibliographical references and index.
   ISBN 978-0-8091-4880-6 (pbk. : alk. paper) — ISBN 978-1-58768-368-8 (ebook)
   1. Bible. Psalms—Introductions. I. Title.
   BS1430.52.A38 2014
   222'.206—dc23
                                                                                      2014013754

ISBN 978-0-8091-4880-6 (paperback)
ISBN 978-1-58768-368-8 (e-book)

Published by Paulist Press
997 Macarthur Boulevard
Mahwah, New Jersey 07430

www.paulistpress.com

Printed and bound in the
United States of America

CONTENTS

Preface vii
Abbreviations ix

Part I: Background to Understanding the Psalms 1

    1. What Is a Psalm? 3
    2. Numbering 3
    3. Collections 5
    4. Titles 7
    5. Classification by Literary Genre 8
    6. The *Sitz im Leben* 9
    7. Date of Composition 9
    8. The Temple Liturgy 10
    9. The Psalter in the Septuagint and Qumran 13
    10. Other Jewish Psalms 15
    11. Relationship to Ancient Poetic Texts 16
    12. Poetic Structure 18
    13. Translation of Hebrew Poetry 23
    14. Theology 26
    15. History of the Interpretation of the Psalms 29
    16. Christian Appropriation 32
    17. Psalms Quoted in the NT 33
    18. Studying the Psalms 35

Part II. Categories of Psalms 49

    1. Individual Supplications 51
        Example: Psalm 6 53

    2. Confidence Psalms 56
        Example: Psalm 3 56

Contents

   3. Public Supplications 59
      Example: Psalm 44 59

   4. Thanksgiving Psalms 64
      Example: Psalm 30 65

   5. Hymns 69
      Example: Psalm 8 70

   6. Zion Psalms 73
      Example: Psalm 122 75

   7. "Yahweh Is King" Psalms 77
      Example: Psalm 47 78

   8. Royal (and Messianic) Psalms 81
      Example: Psalm 2 83

   9. Psalms of the Fidelity of Yahweh 87
      Example: Psalm 95 89

  10. Wisdom Psalms 93
      Example: Psalm 1 95

  11. Different Psalms 98
      Example: Psalm 133 98

Overview of Psalm Classifications 105

The Psalms with Their Proposed Literary Genres 107

Select Bibliography 113
     General Works on the Psalms 113
     Modern Commentaries 115

PREFACE

This book was born as a series of handouts for a course for graduate students. Part 1 presents a survey of general issues related to the study of the Psalms, emphasizing the literary aspects of the text. Part 2 describes the main characteristics of each category of psalms and studies one psalm as an example of each genre.

The classical approach to the Psalms, based on the consideration of their literary genres, receives more attention than the modern canonical or macrostructure approach. This is because at the introductory level, it has been thought more convenient to acquaint students with the characteristics of each individual psalm before trying to relate the psalm with the preceding or successive psalms, as if they were chapters of the Book of Psalms.

In order to use this book as a text for a graduate course, I would suggest that the teacher devote the first and second weeks to the general issues on the Psalms presented in part 1, emphasizing only the most important ideas and leaving to the student the reading of the whole first part for further details. Afterwards, one category of psalms can be studied every week, beginning with a presentation of the general characteristics of the category, an exposition of a psalm as an example of that category, and then, an invitation to the students to prepare, for the following session, the exposition of another psalm of their choice in the same category. This practical exercise will help them to better understand the material presented in class. For the personal presentation, the students should make use of at least one or two academic commentaries (consult the bibliography at the end of this book) and consider the four aspects suggested in this book in the last section of part 1, "18. Studying the Psalms."

The Psalms

I am indebted to many excellent scholars in writing these pages. I have tried as much as possible to refer to the literature that I have consulted or considered as useful, without overloading the text. It is my hope that this concise survey will encourage the reader to study more specialized literature in order to better appreciate the perennial value of the Psalms.

ABBREVIATIONS

AB	Anchor Bible
AER	*American Ecclesiatical Review*
ANET	*Ancient Near Eastern Texts Relating to the OT.* Edited by J. B. Pritchard. 3rd edition. Princeton: Princeton University Press, 1969.
AOTC	Abingdon Old Testament Commentaries
BAC	Biblioteca de autores cristianos
BAR	*Biblical Archeology Review*
Bib	*Biblica*
BibSacra	*Biblioteca Sacra*
BJ	Bible de Jérusalem
BJRL	*Bulletin of the John Rylands Library*
BTB	*Biblical Theological Bulletin*
BZAW	Beihefte zur ZAW
CBQ	*Catholic Biblical Quarterly*
CEC	Critical Eerdmans Commentary
CJT	*Canadian Journal of Theology*
CRBS	*Currents in Research: Biblical Studies*
DJD	Discoveries in the Judean Desert
EBC	The Expositor's Bible Commentary
EstBib	*Estudios Bíblicos*
ExpRev	*Expository Review*
FOTL	The Forms of the Old Testament Literature
HAT	Handbuch zum Alten Testament
HBS	Herders Biblische Studien
HKAT	Handkommentar zum Alten Testament
HSM	Harvard Semitic Monographs
HUCA	*Hebrew Union College Annual*

Int	*Interpretation*
JBLMS	Journal of Biblical Literature Monograph Series
JQR	*Jewish Quarterly Review*
JSOT	*Journal for the Study of the Old Testament*
JSOTSS	Journal for the Study of the Old Testament Supplement Series
JSS	*Journal of Semitic Studies*
KAT	Kommentar zum Alten Testament
NCBC	New Century Bible Commentary
NRSV	New Revised Standard Version
OBS	Österreichische biblische Studien
OTL	Old Testament Library
OTS	*Oudtestamentische Studien*
PL	Patrologia Latina
PTMS	Pittsburgh Theological Monograph Series
RB	*Revue Biblique*
RevExp	*Review and Expositor*
RQ	*Revue de Qumran*
SB	*Subsidia biblica*
SBL	Society of Biblical Literature
SBLDS	Society of Biblical Literature Dissertation Series
SBS	Stuttgarter Bibel Studien
TOTC	Tyndale Old Testament Commentaries
TZ	*Theologische Zeitschrift*
VT	*Vetus Testamentum*
WBC	Word Biblical Commentary
WTJ	*Westminster Theological Journal*
ZAW	*Zeitschrift für die alttestamentliche Wissenschaft*
ZAWNF	*Zeitschrift für die alttestamentliche Wissenschaft Neue Forschung*

PART I

Background to Understanding the Psalms[1]

1. WHAT IS A PSALM?

The word *psalm* comes from the Greek ψαλμός (*psalmos*), which translates the Hebrew word מזמור (*mizmôr*), meaning "song accompanied by a zither." This word appears in the title of seventy-five psalms. In the Hebrew Bible, however, the word that is used to indicate the psalms is the irregular plural תהילים (*tĕhîllîm*) of the word תהיליה (*tĕhîllāh*), which means "praise" (see Ps 145:1); thus the words, ספר תהלם (*sēper tehîllîm*): "Book of Psalms." But in Hebrew, a psalm is also called שיר (*shîr*), "song," a title used in psalms 120—134; and תפלה (*tĕpillāh*), "prayer" or "supplication" (see Ps 72:20). All these titles already reveal the richness of the collection of psalms: they are songs, praise, prayer, and supplication.

We have to be aware that songs and prayers in the Bible are not limited to the Book of Psalms. In fact, we find in the OT poetic fragments written long before the redaction of the Book of Psalms. Among these we have the Song of the Sea (Exod 15:1–18), the Oracles of Balaam (Num 23—24), the Song of Moses (Deut 32), the Blessing of Moses (Deut 33), the Song of Deborah (Judg 5), and the Song of Hannah (1 Sam 2:1–10). From the very beginning, the Israelites wanted to praise in poetry and song the great events of their history of salvation.

2. NUMBERING

The text of the psalms available in modern translations is based on the Hebrew text of Codex Leningradensis B19a, written in AD 1008 by Samuel ben Jacob, a disciple of Aaron ben Asher, of the Tiberias school of Masoretes. This manuscript presents the so-called Masoretic Text (MT) and contains 150 psalms in the Book of Psalms.

However, the Greek version of the Bible, or Septuagint (LXX), and the Latin version (Vulgate, abbreviated Vg)[2] combine some

The Psalms

psalms and separate others: they consider Pss 9 and 10 as one psalm, as also Pss 114 and 115, whereas conversely, they divide both Pss 116 and 147 into two parts. Furthermore, the Septuagint includes Ps 151, which is not considered as canonical, except by the Greek Orthodox Church.

MT (Hebrew)	LXX and Vulgate
1—8	1—8
9—10	9
11—113	10—112
114—115	113
116	114—115
117—146	116—145
147	146—147
148—150	148—150

From this table, one can see that between Ps 10 and Ps 148, the numbering[3] in the LXX/Vg is one unit less in comparison to the MT.

The liturgy has chosen to follow the Vulgate numbering; the modern editions of the Bible follow the MT, putting in parentheses the Vulgate/LXX numbering. The new edition of the Vulgate[4] has preferred to follow the numbering of the MT. We will also follow that of the MT.

Concerning the numbering of verses, there are two systems used in modern versions. The most common system (for example, in the NRSV and the NIV) gives no verse number to the title or superscription of the psalm, so that verse 1 is the first line of the poem. The other system (as in the NAB) follows the use of printed Hebrew Bibles,[5] attributing a verse number to the title or superscription of the psalm. In this second system, the numbering of verses is often one verse ahead the first system. In this book, the NRSV's numbering has been modified to follow this system.

3. COLLECTIONS

In its present form, the Book of Psalms is divided into five collections, each of which ends with a doxology:[6]

Book 1	Pss 1—41	Doxology: Ps 41:13
Book 2	Pss 42—72	Doxology: Ps 72:18-19
Book 3	Pss 73—89	Doxology: Ps 89:52
Book 4	Pss 90—106	Doxology: Ps 106:48
Book 5	Pss 107—149	Final Doxology: Ps 150

This fivefold division suggests that the Jews wanted to compare the Book of Psalms to the Pentateuch, which also has five books,[7] but the Book of Psalms is considered to be not five separate books but a unit.[8] The division into five collections does not seem to be original, however, since it is difficult to find any internal grounds for viewing each of the five books as a self-contained unit.

G. H. Wilson[9] has proposed the idea that the final redactor(s) of the five books of the Psalms gathered the individual psalms with an intentional theological line of thought.[10] He maintains that the first three books (Pss 1—89) present mainly the expectation of and hope for the reestablishment of the Davidic monarchy, and conclude with the acknowledgment of its failure and demise (Ps 89:38-45). But the last two books present the kingship of Yahweh (Pss 93—99), shifting the focus from human kingship to the eternal kingship of Yahweh. Besides, in the last two books, there is an emphasis on the Torah (e.g., Ps 119); this way, wisdom takes precedence over the affliction of the exile and loss of identity, leading to confidence only in God (Pss 144—146). Furthermore, he argues that Pss 1—2 would function as the introduction to the whole Psalter, and Pss 146—150 as its conclusion.

But the situation is not so clear. In fact, Ps 89 ends with a cry to God asking for help and the fulfillment of the promise made to David (Ps 89:49). Besides, the prayer on behalf of the Davidic king is still present in the last two books (e.g., Pss 110; 132; 144). Wilson responds that the person of the king appears only as servant of the kingdom of Yahweh.[11] But the acknowledgment of the lordship of Yahweh over the Davidic king does not diminish the hope and praise for the Davidic monarchy. Morever, the emphasis on the kingship of Yahweh as proposed by Wilson does not explain the great expectation for the coming of the Messiah at the end of the Second Temple period (cf. Ps 110; *Pss. Sol.* 17).

A different view is held by W. Brueggemann, who proposes that the main turning point of the Psalter is not at the end of book 3 but at the end of book 2, with Ps 73 marking a shift from obedience to praise.[12] And C. Westermann notes that individual supplications are more present in the first part of the psalter (Pss 3—41; 51—72), while numerous psalms of praise appear in the second part;[13] accordingly, the shift would be rather from supplication to praise. However, Wilson[14] has pointed out that the model proposed by Brueggemann and Westermann oversimplifies the message of the Psalter.

In any case, other features point to former or earlier collections that precede the postexilic arrangement in five books:

Pss 1—41:	This collection corresponds to the first book of psalms and has three characteristics: the author speaks in first person ("I"), they are attributed to "David,"[15] and refer to God as "Yahweh" (272 times).
Pss 42—49:	Psalms "of the sons of Korah"[16]
Pss 50 and 73—83:	Psalms "of Asaph"
Pss 84—89:	Psalms of Yahweh
Pss 51—72; 101; 103; 108—110; 138—145:	Psalms "of David"[17]
Pss 93; 96—100:	Psalms "Yahweh is King"
Pss 113—118; 135—136; 146—150:	The three "Hallels"[18]
Pss 105—107:	Psalms of the "Historical Creed"[19]
Pss 111—112:	"Wisdom" Alphabetic Psalms
Pss 120—134:	Psalms of Ascents (to Jerusalem)

Background to Understanding the Psalms

4. TITLES

The way of grouping the psalms mentioned above (e.g., "Psalms of David," "Psalms of Asaph") derives mainly from information provided in the title of the psalms. In fact, the titles give us the following information (most of the time difficult for us to understand):[20]

1. The literary genre according to ancient and sometimes unknown categories: "psalm" (מזמור, *mizmôr*) (fifty-seven times; Pss 3—6; 8—9; 12—13; 15; etc.), "song" (שׁיר, *shîr*) (thirty times; Pss 45; 48; 65—68; etc.), "wisdom text" (משׂכיל *maśkîl*) (thirteen times; Pss 32; 42; 44—45; 55; etc.), "allusion" (מכתם *mikttam*) (six times; Pss 16; 56—60), "prayer" (תפלה *tĕpillāh*) (five times; Pss 17; 86; 90; 102; 142), "prayer" (תהלה, *tĕhîllāh*) (once; Ps 145).
2. The way in which the psalm is played or performed: a) the kind of instrument to be used for the psalm: "for strings" (בנגינות *binegînôt*) (Pss 4; 6), "for flute" (אל־הנחילות *ʾel hannĕḥîlôt*) (Ps 5), etc.; b) the tone or mode: "for soprano" (על־עלמות *ʿal ʿălāmôt*) (Ps 46), "low tone" (על־השׁמינית *ʿal hashemînît*) (Ps 6), etc.; c) the way in which it is played: "to the manner of Jeduthun" (על־ידותון *ʿal yĕdûtûn*) (Ps 62), "afflicted" (על־מחלת *ʿal māḥălat*) (Ps 53), "to the doe of the dawn" (על־אילת *ʿal ʾayelet*) (Ps 22), "lilies" (על־שׁשׁנים *ʿal shōshanîm*) (Ps 45), and so on.

    Here it is convenient to note the frequent use of the Hebrew word סלה *selāh* in the Psalms (seventy-one times).[21] Its etymology and meaning is uncertain, but it seems to have a musical significance, either in regard to the singing or recitation of the psalm, or with respect to the music accompanying the psalm. The most accepted translation is "pause" or "silence," given the fact that the Greek translators used the word διάψαλμα, *diapsalma*, which might be taken to imply "pause" or "instrumental interlude."[22] Another interpretation is to understand *selāh* in the sense of "always" (Jerome: *semper*), indicating a reference to a doxology (for example, *per omnia saecula saeculorum* in the liturgy).

3. The liturgical use: "For the Sabbath" (Ps 92), "In commemoration" [of the new year?] (Ps 38), "For thanksgiving" (Ps 100), "At the end of the Feast of the Tabernacles" (Ps 29; title added in the LXX), and so on.
4. Allusion to historical circumstances: the time when David was persecuted by Saul (Pss 7; 34; 52; 56; 59), when David was saved from all his enemies (Ps 18), the sin of David (Ps 51), and so on.
5. The author of the psalm: seventy-three psalms are attributed to David[23] (Pss 61; 62, etc.); two psalms to Solomon (Pss 72; 127); twelve to Asaph[24] (Pss 73—83); eleven to the sons of Korah[25] (Pss 44—49); one each to Heman (Ps 88), Ethan (Ps 89), and Moses (Ps 90).

These headings however, present a number of difficulties that hinder us from using them as an adequate system of identification; they have a limited utility for group classification.[26]

5. CLASSIFICATION BY LITERARY GENRE

It seems that the most suitable form of grouping the psalms for our purposes of study, as well as for pastoral work and prayer, is to classify them according to particular and precise literary genres. The foundational work for this classification was done by Hermann Gunkel[27] (1862–1932), who considered the following criteria for classifying the psalms: a) the theme, b) the structure of the psalm, c) literary or stylistic characteristics, and d) the *Sitz im Leben* or setting in life in which the psalm was created. Gunkel proposed five major classifications or categories: hymns, public lamentations, royal psalms, individual lamentations, and individual thanksgiving psalms.

A more developed classification followed Gunkel's pattern:[28] individual supplications, confidence psalms, public supplications, thanksgiving psalms, hymns, royal (messianic) psalms, Zion psalms, psalms Yahweh-is-King, psalms of the fidelity of Yahweh (historical meditations), wisdom psalms, and different prayers.

While this classification is in no way definitive, it will serve as the basis from which we will study the message of the psalms.

6. THE *SITZ IM LEBEN*

The consideration of the setting in life (German: *Sitz im Leben*) in which each specific psalm was composed has remained an important issue discussed among scholars, since the identification of such a context can better facilitate the understanding of the message of the psalm. For example, was Ps 8 composed for liturgical use in the temple of Jerusalem? Or was it composed for the use of Jewish communities in the exile? Or for private use?

The task of determining the living context is not easy, however, since the psalms offer few indications that can indicate with certainty a precise historical or geographical circumstance. Moreover, most of the psalms underwent further elaboration after the exile, and the late additions or modifications of the text can mislead the scholar in attributing a specific historical context. So, for example, the information provided by the title that appears in 116 psalms frequently reveals a late adaptation of the original psalm.

7. DATE OF COMPOSITION

The date of a psalm is very difficult to determine. Some scholars have proposed giving them an ancient date and, as place of origin, Jerusalem, because of the abundant use of the name Yahweh for God:

	"Yahweh"	"Elohim"
Book 1	272 times	15 times
Book 2	30 times	164 times
Book 3	44 times	43 times
Book 4	103 times	0 times
Book 5	236 times	7 times

But the use of the divine name as a method of dating the psalms seems an insufficient criterion. What we can say is that the psalms come from a variety of periods, from before the monarchy to after the exile. Probably the Book of Psalms substantially attained its present form by the fourth century BC. To establish their date of composition more precisely, we have to consider each psalm individually and pay attention to their ideas and motifs, their titles, language, and literary structure.

So, for example, M. First has recently proposed considering the alphabetic[29] Ps 34 as originally written before the exile. His proposal is based on the fact that in inverting the order of some verses (vv. 17, 16, 18), the text makes theological sense: God listens (v. 18), to the cry of the righteous (v. 16), not to the cry of the evildoers (v. 17). This rearrangement of verses produces a reversal of the Hebrew letters ע *'ayin* – פ *pē* (vv. 16–17). However, First holds that while the order *'ayin – pē* was the standard order after the exile, some ancient preexilic abecedaries indicate an order *pē – 'ayin*.[30]

8. THE TEMPLE LITURGY

Given the fact that the psalms are closely associated with the liturgy in the temple of Jerusalem,[31] we should say something about this liturgy, even though the theme is complicated and our knowledge on this issue is limited.[32]

We have no information about the pre-Davidic Temple in Jerusalem, except that Genesis 14:18–20 mentions the name of Melchizedek, king of Salem, that is, Jerusalem (Ps 76:3), and priest of El-Elyon, who seems to have been a Canaanite god. In this case, Yahweh would have taken the place of this pagan deity, as well as his titles (cf. Pss 18:14; 47:3; 97:9; Gen 24:3). And for some authors, the Israelite temple of Jerusalem would have taken the place of the Canaanite temple.[33]

While David was busy throughout his life with many wars, his son Solomon began the construction of the temple in the fourth year of his kingship and ended in the eleventh year (1 Kgs 6:37–38). The description of the Solomonic temple is provided in

1 Kings 6—7 and 2 Chronicles 3—4, but in many places the description is difficult to understand. The temple was comprised of three main sections: *Ulam* (atrium), *Hekal* (holy), and *Debir* (holy of holies), measuring a total of 35 m long by 10 m wide by 15 m high.[34] The tripartite structure of the temple is also seen in other temples, such as the Canaanite temple at Tell Tainat in Syria (ninth century BC), or the Israelite temple at Arad. The Solomonic temple was part of the king's palace (as was the case also in Assyrian palaces), but there was a public gate to the temple court so that worshipers did not have to pass through the palace. On each side of the porch, there was a massive bronze pillar with the names of *Yakin* ("he will establish") and *Boaz* ("in strength").

The holy of holies, which contained the ark of the covenant, was entered only once a year by the high priest, during the feast of the Day of Atonement (Heb 9:7). The holy, which could be entered only by priests (Heb 9:6), contained utensils for the cult, such as the golden altar of incense, the table of showbread, and ten lampstands.[35] A veil separated the holy of holies from the holy.[36] The atrium was divided into three subsections: the atrium of the priests (*ezrat kohanim*), the atrium for male worshipers (*ezrat yisrael*), and the atrium for female worshipers (*ezrat našim*). It was in the atrium that public prayers and songs were sung, either accompanying the sacrifices or worshiping God. However, prayers and songs were also sung outside the atrium, as the crowds were entering the temple compound. The temple had its own singers and musicians.

The sacrifice provided by the people and offered on their behalf by the priests took place in the atrium and was the most important act of the Israelite cult, being accompanied by prayers that frequently, because it was public prayer, were sung and accompanied by musical instruments (Amos 5:22–23). A number of psalms make reference to this sacrificial cult of the temple (Pss 20:3–4; 26:6–8; 27:6; 66:13–15; 107:22; 116:17) and even mention the temple, where they were sung (Pss 48:10; 65:5; 96:6, 8; 118:26; 134:1; 135:1–2). Some psalms were composed for the time when pilgrims were going up to the temple (Pss 120—134 have the title "Psalms of Ascents").

Furthermore, during the celebration of the liturgical feasts, processions were accompanied by prayers and songs. In this sense, the title added to Ps 29 (28) in the Greek (LXX) indicates that this psalm was sung during the last day of the Feast of the Tabernacles (*Sukkot*),[37] and other psalms refer to processions probably related to the same feast (Pss 95:1–2, 6; 118:19–20, 26–27; Deut 31:11).[38] The title of Ps 30, "Canticle for the Dedication of the House," indicates that this psalm was composed for the commemoration of the purification of the temple by Judas Maccabaeus in 165 BC (1 Macc 4:52–54).[39] Pss 113—118; 136;[40] and 146—150 formed the *Hallel* (hymn of praise) sung at the beginning and at the end of the Passover supper (cf. Matt 26:30; Mark 14:26).

The main feasts or festivals were *Rosh Ha-shanah* (New Year), *Yom Kippur* (Day of Atonement), *Sukkot* (Feast of Tabernacles), *Hanukkah* (Feast of Dedication of the Temple), *Pesah* (Passover),[41] and *Shavuot* (Feast of Weeks or Firstfruits or Pentecost).[42] But prayers and songs were also sung during other ceremonies, such as the enthronement of the new king, or in case of war or disasters. The title of Ps 92, "For the Sabbath," indicates that this psalm was recited during that special day of prayer.

During the day, at the temple, there was a morning service (Ps 5) and an afternoon service (Ps 4; Jdt 9:1). But pious worshippers used to pray three times a day (Ps 55:18; Dan 6:11). The Israelites used to pray standing up (1 Sam 1:9, 26; Jer 18:20) but also kneeling or prostrate (1 Kgs 8:54–55; Isa 45:23; Dan 6:11; Pss 5:8; 95:6; 99:5, 9).[43] Some people also extended their hands to heaven (1 Kgs 8:22, 54; Ps 28:2; Isa 1:15).

The main ministrants of the temple were the priests (descendants of Zadok)[44] and the Levites, the latter assisting the priests in the daily service while assuming the functions of singers, gatekeepers, and servants. The entire priesthood was divided into twenty-four groups who took weekly turns. Each priestly group had a corresponding group of Levites and a group of lay Israelites representing the entire people.[45]

Psalms were probably sung either antiphonally (between two groups of singers) or responsorially (between the soloist and the congregations). Some psalms were sung as litanies, with a recurring short response repeated by the laypeople after phrases sung by a soloist or a group of Levites. In the second temple (see below), the choir consisted of twelve Levites, according to Mishnaic tradition.[46] In addition to this, psalms were also sung in synagogues, without the use of musical instruments. The singing of psalms, chanting of Scripture, and singing of prayers comprised the music in synagogues, performed by the precentor and congregation, or antiphonally by two groups of congregations (*Sukkah* 38b).

The Solomonic temple was destroyed in 587 BC by Nebuchadnezzar, king of Babylon. After the exile, the temple was rebuilt by Zerubbabel, the governor of Davidic line, and the high priest Joshua (520–515 BC). However, this second temple was only a shadow of the glory of the first temple. The Zadokite line of priests resumed its high priestly role at this time. With the social reform of Nehemiah (445–433 BC), and above all the religious reform of Ezra, who was a descendant of the high priest and "a scribe skilled in the law of Moses" (Ezra 7:6) (398 BC),[47] the temple liturgy received a vigorous renewal. Most probably, it was at Ezra's time that the final collection of the five books of the psalms was made, together with the edition of the five books of the Pentateuch.[48]

In 20 BC, Herod the Great began a major renovation of the whole temple complex, building a large esplanade measuring 490 m x 320 m. It was this temple that was visited by Jesus and his disciples.

9. THE PSALTER IN THE SEPTUAGINT AND QUMRAN

In addition to the different numbering, the collection of psalms that we have in the Hebrew Bible presents other differences in comparison to the collection in the Septuagint and in the Qumran Psalms scrolls.

The LXX adds titles to eleven psalms, attributing them to David. This happens mainly within the family of "Yahweh is King" psalms (Pss 93; 96—99), or psalms of "the fidelity of Yahweh" (Ps 95).[49] Furthermore, the LXX adds ten historical notices in the titles of the psalms of David. Consequently, the LXX gives emphasis to David and the Davidic covenant.[50]

Concerning the Psalter at Qumran, there are thirty-seven scrolls containing the text, complete or in part, of 126 psalms of the Hebrew Bible. Therefore, the Book of the Psalms is the most attested biblical book in the Qumran scrolls.

Two scrolls are particularly important because of their size: 4QPs^a (or 4Q83) and 11QPs^a (or 11Q5). In these scrolls, it is notable that from Ps 1 up to Ps 89, the psalms appear in the same order as in the Hebrew Bible, with twenty psalms missing.[51] But after Ps 89, there are major differences: some psalms are missing, the order is different, the text itself has different readings,[52] and other psalms not included in the Hebrew Bible are incorporated.

The most important scroll is 11QPs^a, also called "the Psalms Scroll of Qumran,"[53] because of its size (a. 4 meters). The scroll contains thirty-nine biblical psalms from books 4 and 5, nine other psalms or hymns not included in the Hebrew Bible, and one prose composition on David, in the following order:[54] Pss 101—103; 109; 118; 104; 147; 105; 146; 148; 121—132; 119; 135—136; *catena*; 145; *154*; *Plea for deliverance*; 139; 137—138; *Sirach 51*; *Apostrophe to Zion*; 93; 41; 133; 144; *155*; 142—143; 149—150; *Hymn to the Creator*; 2 Sam 23:1–7; *The compositions by David*; 140; 134; *151A*; *151B*.

So, the content of the Psalter at Qumran is different from the one in the Hebrew Bible, mainly regarding Books 4 and 5 (Pss 90—150).[55] Therefore, it is more appropriate to say that there were different collections of psalms at Qumran, in addition to the one adopted in the Hebrew Bible (MT).[56]

From the theological point of view, in the Qumran Psalter there is an important omission of the "Yahweh is King" psalms (Pss 94—100) as well as the wisdom-tinged Hallelujah psalms (Pss 110—117). On the other hand, eleven texts not included in the Hebrew Bible, but incorporated in 11QPs^a, add considerable emphasis to the person of David. This is reinforced by the fact that non-Davidic psalms are omitted as well. Consequently, the Davidic king plays an important role in the Qumran Psalms Scroll.[57]

From the point of view of the text, the manuscripts from Qumran offer also some interesting readings. For example, 11QPs^a (or

11Q5 Col. XVII) contains a verse of Ps 145 that is not attested in the Masoretic Text, verse 13b: "Yahweh is trustworthy in all his words, and upright in all his deeds." This verse begins in Hebrew with the letter *nun*, נ, one of the twenty-two letters of the Hebrew alphabet. Now, Ps 145 is an acrostic psalm, meaning that each verse of it begins with one of the letters of the Hebrew alphabet, but the text of Ps 145 according to the MT misses the letter *nun*, which should be between verse 13 and verse 14. Therefore, it is usually thought that this verse was lost in the Masoretic tradition, but now it has been recovered thanks to the testimony of one of the manuscripts found at Qumran (which is attested also in the Septuagint text and the Syriac version). Nowadays, verse 13b of Ps 145 is usually included in modern Bibles.

Finally, it should be mentioned that at Qumran there are also some commentaries or "pesher" (plural: "pesharim") to the Psalms. These commentaries consider the psalms together with other biblical books, as in the case of 4QFlorilegium[58] (or 4Q174), or some particular psalms alone, such as 1 QpPs (or 1Q16) commenting on parts of Pss 57 and 68, or 4QpPs^a (or 4Q171) commenting on parts of Pss 37, 45, and 60. These commentaries actualize the biblical texts, interpreting them in the light of the events of their own time.

10. OTHER JEWISH PSALMS[59]

In addition to the 150 psalms in the Hebrew Bible, there are six other apocryphal psalms attributed to David found elsewhere: Ps 151 (which originally was two psalms: Pss 151A and 151B) is found in the LXX; Pss 152 and 153 are preserved only in the Syriac Peshitta; Pss 154 and 155 are available in Hebrew (Dead Sea Scrolls: 11QPs^a) and the Syriac Peshitta. The importance of these psalms is that they reveal that the definition of the canonical psalms prior to AD 70 (the occupation of Qumran by the Roman legions) was not yet achieved.[60]

The eighteen *Psalms of Solomon*, which are not part of the Bible, are available in some copies of the LXX and the Syriac Peshitta. The attribution to Solomon is perhaps due to the similarity between *Pss. Sol.* 17 and Ps 72 ("Of Solomon"); another possible reason would be the attempt to emphasize their value. It has usually been thought that they were composed within the Pharisaic circle,[61] although a second good possibility is an Essene community.[62] While the biblical psalms refer vaguely to their historical context, the *Psalms of Solomon* refer specifically to their historical context, reflecting the turbulent period of the Roman occupation, and incite to rebellion. The most interesting is *Pss. Sol.* 17, because it contains a messianic hymn.

11. RELATIONSHIP TO ANCIENT POETIC TEXTS[63]

The psalms in the Bible, especially the hymns, prayers, and laments, retain some similarities with other poetic texts of ancient Near Eastern cultures, as well as important differences. The oldest texts come from the Sumerian, Akkadian, Egyptian, and Canaanite cultures, as most of them were written around the second millennium BC.

It must be noted that the similarities between biblical psalms and ancient Near Eastern poetic texts are due to a common poetic background, the religious character of the texts, and their cultic setting. A direct influence on individual psalms is, on the other hand, dubious. The most debated cases are Ps 29 and the Ugaritic prayer to El,[64] and perhaps also Ps 104 and the Egyptian sun hymn of Akhenaton.[65]

In the first case, there are certainly strikingly similar expressions (e.g., "sons of God," Ps 29:1; "Lebanon…Sirion…," Ps 29:6; "Yahweh sits enthroned as king forever," Ps 29:10, translation modified), but more than supposing a direct influence,[66] Cazelles points out that Ps 29 appears as a rereading of the Canaanite text.[67] Furthermore, Castellino[68] notices that the praise of the voice of a god is not uncommon in the ancient Near East, and, therefore, it is no surprise that the psalmist in Israel decided to praise Yahweh's voice in Ps 29.

In the second case, G. Nagel[69] has pointed out that the similarity of Ps 104 to Genesis 1 is so close as to exclude the need to look for an Egyptian parallel. Besides, an essential difference is that in the hymn to Akhenaton, the sun god's providence is limited to daytime, and during the night evil forces prevail; but in Ps 104 the night is also part of God's creation (Ps 104:19–20). Furthermore, a direct influence is to be excluded because of the different themes in both texts: in the hymn to Akhenaton, the dominant theme is the sun, but in Ps 104 the sun plays a secondary role.

While ruling out a direct influence of these ancient texts upon the Psalms, an important thing that we can learn from those texts is that hymns, prayers, and laments from Egypt and Mesopotamia, originally composed for a cultic setting, were easily adapted to other situations. For example, Egyptian cultic laments were adapted as private funerary texts; or Mesopotamian laments for temple construction were eventually used in vigils against divine anger.[70] Hence, we have to be aware that individual supplication psalms most probably were used in other contexts. So for example, Sparks points out the conclusion of Ps 69, in which verses 34 through 36 give a collective tone to this individual supplication.[71] Or, the title of Ps 92, which marks the psalm for use during the Sabbath, even when nothing in the text refers to such an occasion.[72]

Another thing that we learn from Mesopotamian and Hittite prayers and laments is their close connection with ritual sacrifices and offerings. We can suppose that the same is true of the psalms in the Bible, even when only few of them allude to such ritual votive offerings (Pss 51:9, 21; 54:8; 56:13; 61:6; 65:2).[73]

Last, it should be noted that the psalms of the Fidelity of Yahweh (e.g., Pss 105—106) do not have a parallel with ancient texts from the Near East. On the other hand, hymns or prayers worshiping kings in the Near East (Egypt, Ur), do not have a parallel in the biblical psalms; the same is true of divination prayers (Mesopotamia) or prayers to secure a blessed afterlife (Egyptian funerary texts).[74] This situation shows the unique dimension of the faith of Israel.

12. POETIC STRUCTURE[75]

In order to understand the message of the Psalms, it is important to know the basics of the literary genre of poetry, since all the Psalms were written as poetry. Other books of the OT also appear in poetic form: Proverbs, Job, Canticles, Lamentations, Sirach, and Wisdom, and large sections of the books of Isaiah, Jeremiah, Ezekiel, and the minor prophets were written in poetry. Furthermore, we find songs and pieces of songs embedded in the historical books of the OT (e.g., Deut 32).

Hebrew poetry seems to be based on three pillars: parallelism, meter or rhythm, and strophe. While we know a lot about parallelism thanks to the contribution of R. Lowth (1753),[76] we know little about meter and almost nothing about strophes. The problem is that there are no works of ancient Israel, comparable to those extant from the classical world (e.g., Aristotle, *De Poetica*) that explain the nature of poetics and rhetoric.

PARALLELISM

The most characteristic feature of Hebrew poetry is the use of parallelism.[77] It consists of the repetition of an idea in synonymous, antithetic, or complementary terms.

In *synonymous parallelism*, the same idea is repeated with equivalent terms so that further clarity or expansion is achieved. In *antithetic parallelism*, the second member opposes a contrary idea to the first one, thereby giving to the idea of the whole verse better comprehension and emphasis. In *complementary parallelism*, the second member completes and develops the idea of the first member.

Example of synonymous parallelism (Ps 114:1):[78]

| When Israel | went out | from Egypt |
| the house of Jacob | | from a people of strange language, |

Sometimes the synonym is presented in a broad sense and not in a strict one. So for example, in Ps 150:1:

```
Praise God      in his sanctuary
praise him      in his mighty firmament!
```

In the second line, there is no correspondence between "his sanctuary" and "his mighty firmament"; the psalmist wants to affirm that the praise to God cannot be confined to an earthly building.[79] Some authors prefer to call this particular form of synonymous parallelism *climactic parallelism*.

It has to be noted also that sometimes synonymous parallelism appears in a chiastic or crossed form. For example in Ps 58:7:

```
Let them vanish ⤫ like water that runs away
      like grass    let them be trodden down and wither.
```

Example of antithetic or contrasting parallelism (Ps 20:8):

```
They      will collapse and fall,
but we    shall rise and stand upright.
```

The antithetic parallelism can also be presented in a chiastic form, as for example in Ps 1:6:

```
For the LORD         watches over ⤫ the way of the righteous
          but the way of the wicked    will perish,
```

or in Prov 11:11:

```
By the blessing of the upright ⤫ a city is exalted
          but it is overthrown      by the mouth of the wicked
```

Example of synthetic, complementary, or constructive parallelism (Ps 19:7):[80]

```
The law of the LORD is perfect,
          reviving the soul
```

The synthetic parallelism can also be presented in a "step" or "staircase" form, as, for example, in Ps 94:1:

The Psalms

> O LORD,   you God of vengeance,
>   you God of vengeance,   shine forth![81]

These parallelisms can be found in mixed forms. A very good example is Isaiah 1:2–3, in which the three kinds of parallelism occur:[82]

> *a*   Hear, O heavens, and listen, O earth;
> *b*   For the LORD has spoken:
> *c*   I reared children and brought them up,
> *d*   but they have rebelled against me.
> *e*   The ox knows its owner,
> *f*   And the donkey its master's crib;
> *g*   But Israel does not know,
> *h*   my people does not understand.

Here *a* contains complementary parallelism; *a-b* is a complementary distich, or pair of verse lines; *c-d* is an antithetic distich; *e-f* and *g-h* are synonymous distiches; but *e-f* and *g-h* are antithetic to each other.

The concept of parallelism is a useful tool for understanding the meaning of some words by means of their relationship to other known words in a parallel structure. The use of this literary figure helps to make the meaning of some terms or expressions more precise; it makes it easier to remember some ideas and also gives special emphasis to those ideas.[83]

METER AND RHYTHM

The use of meter or rhythm in Hebrew poetry has been greatly debated throughout the centuries.[84] The theories based on the vocalization of the Masoretic Text have been criticized on the basis that they do not represent the pronunciation of the poetry in its original form and the original form is represented only by the consonantal text.

If we consider rhythm as the pattern of recurrent strong and weak accents, vocalization, and silence in speech, we can suppose that meter in Hebrew poetry was reckoned in terms of accented syllables.[85] In this case, the most important meters were 3 + 3 and 3 + 2:[86]

> 3 + 3: He comes fórth like a flówer and wíthers,
> he flées like a shádow and contínues not
> Job 14:2 (translation modified)
>
> 3 + 2: The Lórd has scórned his áltar
> disówned his sánctuary
> Lam 2:7

Other meters are: 4 + 4, 2 + 2, and 4 + 3. However, it must be noted that the use of a metrical pattern is not rigidly observed.

STROPHES

While strophes are used in classical poetry, the use of strophes or stanzas seems to have been used only occasionally in Hebrew poetry. In the English translation of the psalms, however, a kind of strophic structure is used based on units of meaning or recurrence of a refrain; so, for example, the repetition of a phrase in Ps 107 ("Let them thank Yahweh for his faithful love, for his wonders for the children of Adam," vv. 8, 15, 21, 31 [my translation]). And it is clear that some of the alphabetic psalms are strophic in form, as, for example, Ps 118, where the first eight verses begin with the letter *'alep* (א), the second eight verses with *bet* (ב), and so on.[87]

OTHER SECONDARY FEATURES IN HEBREW POETRY

- The alphabetic acrostic: each verse (Pss 25; 34), hemistich (half a line of verse) (Pss 9—10), or alternate verse (Ps 37) begins with a new letter of the alphabet. Sometimes two or more verses begin with the same letter (Ps 119).

- Repetition: duplication of some words or ideas for the sake of emphasis (Pss 22:1; 27:14; 130:6)
- Refrain: repetition of a verse (Ps 42:6, 12)
- *Responsio*: similar sound or idea at the beginning of each strophe (Pss 136; 148)
- *Concatenatio*: when the end of a strophe is linked to the beginning of the following, by means of the repetition of a word (hook word). This literary figure can also be found between different psalms.[88]
- *Inclusio*: delimitation of a strophe by means of repetition of words or ideas at the beginning and end of a strophe or section (Ps 122:7-8).[89] This literary figure can also be found as gathering a whole group of psalms.[90]
- Rhyme: similar sound of the endings of verses (Ps 96:4b, 5a)[91]
- Alliteration: repetition of the same letter or syllable at the beginning of successive words (Isa 14:22d)[92]
- Paronomasia: repetition of words similar in sound (Ps 122:6)[93]

The use of these literary features has to be taken into account for a proper understanding of the text. Many times these features take priority over the plain theological meaning; that is, sometimes the word that it is used may not be the best where the meaning is concerned, but the author uses it because of the rhyme of the text; consequently, some words have to be understood more because of stylistic reasons than because of their actual meaning.

METAPHORS

Another literary feature in Hebrew poetry to keep in mind is the abundant use of metaphors. In a metaphor, one thing or idea is compared to another, owing to some association or connection, based on use or effects or quality or character. Unlike the simile, in which one thing is said to be "like" another or "resembles" another, in the metaphor it is said that one thing "is" another thing, or "represents" it. Consequently, the metaphor appeals to our imagination or feelings,[94] unlike the simile, which appeals to our intelligence.

The use of metaphors in the Psalms is abundant, being used in reference either to God (e.g., God as "rock" appears twenty-one times; as "fortress" appears six times; as "shield" appears fourteen times) or to the people (e.g., the individual as a "worm" in Ps 22:7; the whole people as "flock" ready for slaughter in Ps 74:1).

Furthermore, regarding metaphors, it must also be noted that in Hebrew there is no copula uniting or identifying the subject with the predicate in a sentence, as is the case in English with the copula of the verb "to be." Therefore, in Hebrew we read, for example, in Ps 23:1: "Yahweh my Shepherd" (יהוה רעי, *Yahweh rō'î*), but in English we translate it as "The LORD *is* my shepherd."

On the other hand, in similes the Hebrew usually uses the letter *kāp* (כ) to indicate a similitude or resemblance. So, for example, in Ps 92:12 we read, "The righteous flourish *like* the palm tree" (צדיק כתמר יפרח, *ṣaddîq kattāmār yiprāḥ*).

13. TRANSLATION OF HEBREW POETRY

A quick comparison of modern English Bibles will show major differences in the translation of the psalms. This is due not only to the criteria adopted by the editors regarding the specific audience for which the Bible is addressed (e.g., whether the translation is intended for children, for liturgical singing, for study, etc.), or problems of textual criticism (e.g., the existence of variant readings due to human error in the copy process of manuscripts), but to our limited knowledge of biblical Hebrew.

THE USE OF TENSES

It is generally accepted that biblical Hebrew has two tenses, the imperfect (usually to describe the present or future) and the perfect (usually to describe the past). However, it is incorrect to think of these two as tenses in the way that classical languages express distinctions in time with respect to actions or states.[95] It seems better to consider the two forms as primarily defining the aspect of an action or state, and not time. While the so-called perfect tense (better to call it *qatal*) usually indicates completed action, the so-called imperfect tense (better to call it *yiqtol*) indicates incomplete action.[96] The *qatal* appears as a suffixed verb and the *yiqtol* appears as a prefixed verb. But this situation is complicated by the presence of the waw-conversive,[97] which appears to transform the *qatal* into a *yiqtol*, and vice versa, once the waw-conversive is prefixed to the verbal form.[98]

These rules seem to work in Hebrew narrative most of the time; but in Hebrew poetry (e.g., the psalms) no rule satisfactorily explains the use of the forms of the verb. In practice, the context is the principal guide to determining the most appropriate translation, assisted by a comparison with the translation offered by ancient versions (e.g., Greek, Latin). But the consideration of context in poetical texts is generally open to ambiguity, so that the translator is working partially in the dark with respect to translation of Hebrew verbs in poetry.

THE LACK OF VOWELS

Ancient biblical Hebrew, like modern Hebrew, was written without vowels, and it was up to the reader to supply the vowels while reading the consonantal text. In some cases, it was possible to read the same word in two different ways (for example, in English the consonants *rd* can be related to the words *red* or *read* or *reed*), and it was the context that helped the reader to infer the correct reading.

To facilitate the correct reading of the biblical text, a group of Jewish scribes and scholars called the Masoretes added vowels to the consonantal text between the seventh and tenth centuries AD in Israel and Babylon. Their vocalized text has been preserved up to our days and is referred to as the Masoretic Text. Although the Masoretes lived in a time when biblical Hebrew had ceased to be spoken, most scholars believe that their understanding of biblical Hebrew was pretty accurate.

There are some passages in the Hebrew Bible, however, where the reading of the Masoretes seems not to be adequate, and scholars propose other alternative readings of the consonantal text. Now, depending on the reading adopted, the meaning of the text can be greatly modified. For example, in Ps 4:2 we have the consonants *'nny*, which were vocalized by the Masoretes as *'anēnî*, which is the imperative "hear me." But the Jewish translators of the Greek Bible (LXX) understood the vocalization to be *'ananî*, which is the past tense "heard me," since they used the Greek word εἰσήκουσεν (*eisēkousen*). Jerome, who translated the Hebrew Bible into Latin, also understood the word *'nny* as *'ananî*, "heard me," since he used the Latin words *exaudivit me* in the Vulgate (and not *exaudi me*). Now, this different vocalization changes the meaning of the text:

Ps 4:2 (MT) "When I call, *hear me*, O God"
Ps 4:2 (LXX; Vg) "When I called, God *heard me*"

Following the reading of the Masoretes (MT), Psalm 4 appears as a supplication psalm; but following the reading of the Septuagint (LXX) and the Vulgate (Vg), Psalm 4 appears as a confidence psalm or a thanksgiving psalm.[99]

UNKNOWN WORDS

To the difficulty of understanding Hebrew syntax, one has to add the problem of morphology concerning words that appear only once in the Bible (the so-called *hapax legomena*) and whose meaning is not clear at all. These *hapax legomena* are abundant in poetry.

14. THEOLOGY[100]

The Book of Psalms gathers a wide variety of Jewish theological ideas on God, creation, humankind, history, society, and other subjects. All major theological trends that developed in ancient Israel have left their footprint in the psalms. The beliefs in one God, in the election of Israel, in the covenant, in the judgment, and in the expectation of the coming of the Messiah are all present in the psalms. Therefore, the study of the psalms allows us to have a unique window into the theological thinking and belief of ancient Israel.

The theology of the psalms is very rich. A better appraisal would take into account the different categories of psalms (this will be done below). However, here we can mention three major theological characteristics of the psalms, taking them as a whole. The theology of the psalms can be grouped under three aspects.

HUMANKIND IN ITS RELATIONSHIP TO GOD

Several categories of psalms focus on the attitude of humans in regard to God.

- Four psalm categories—individual supplications, confidence psalms, public supplications, and thanksgiving psalms—portray a vivid attitude of humankind toward God.

    In these psalms, among the different situations in which humanity is described, the situation of being under test is particularly notable: sickness, disaster, persecution, religious temptation. The answers to these situations are a) acknowledgment of being a sinner and asking forgiveness of God (Ps 51); b) consciousness of not having sinned against God, and therefore protests for innocence and appeals to God's righteousness (Pss 7; 17; 26; 59); c) full confidence in God, even if danger or temptations surround the individual (Ps 23); and d) distress because of

the situation, hate against the enemy, and hope in God (these are the imprecatory psalms: Pss 69; 109, etc.).
- The wisdom psalms convey a more speculative description of humanity's attitude in its relationship to God. They praise the law and the benefits of keeping it (Pss 1; 15) or the bad consequences of transgressing it (Ps 52).

GOD IN HIS WONDERFUL BEHAVIOR IN CREATION AND HISTORY

The praise of God, his attributes, and his creative power are portrayed in the hymns. They sing the power and majesty of God in creation (Ps 19); the heavens and sun are glorious signs of God's wisdom and power (Ps 29). The creative power of God (Pss 90:2; 89:12) is the main characteristic of God in contrast to the idols (Ps 115:3-4). Among all the creatures, a special place is given to humanity (Ps 8). Among the many attributes of God are his omniscience and omnipresence (Ps 139). The anthropomorphisms used in regard to God are to be considered as rhetorical devices enabling the individual to talk about God.

GOD IN HIS SAVING ACTIVITY

The saving action of God takes shape in the figure of the Messiah, God's "chosen one." Messianism is the kingship of God over redeemed humanity, who is subjected to God by means of the one sent by him, the Messiah, in the time designated by God. The royal (or messianic) psalms mainly present this idea.

Two groups of people frequently mentioned in the psalms are the poor and the enemies.

THE POOR[101]

In over forty psalms, the psalmist is described as "poor" (e.g., Pss 40:17; 70:5; 86:1; 109:22) and appeals to God as savior of the poor (e.g., Pss 12:5; 14:6; 34:6); the king appointed by God is also addressed as defender of the poor (e.g., Ps 72:4, 12).[102] The poor person (עני, *'ānî*; עגו, *'ānāw*)[103] is someone who is defenseless (cf. Ps 72:12) and therefore in need (cf. Ps 86:1 "I am poor and needy")[104] or in affliction. While in early times the poor denoted a social condition indicating poverty and distress (cf. Exod 22:25; Lev 23:22; Deut 24:12), a moral or religious meaning was given later, especially after the exile, so that the "poor of Yahweh" denoted the people faithful to God (cf. Ps 37:14). Kittel[105] has proposed to explain the development of the meaning of the term on the basis of different causes: the preaching of the prophets defending the cause of the poor (Isa 3:14), and the fact that the pious (הסידים *ḥăsîdîm*) Jews became poor in the exile.

In the psalms, the poor people (ענוים, *'ănāwîm*) are those who know that their cause is in the hands of God and only God can save them (Pss 34:7; 56:3). Hence, the word *poor* designates an attitude of the soul.[106] Therefore, the "poor" sometimes appear together with the "just ones" (צדיקים, *ṣaddîqîm*), and the "saints" (קדשים, *qedōshîm*).[107]

THE ENEMY[108]

The "poor" in the psalms appear persecuted by the "enemies" (אויב, *'ôyēb*), "evildoers" (פעלי און, *pō'ălē 'āwen*), and "wicked" (רשעים *reshāîm*). The identity of the enemies depends on who is the subject speaking in the psalm: a private individual ("I"), a group of people ("we"), the leader of a group or nation ("the king"). But the situation is even more complicated since it seems that in some cases, the "I" stands for the community. Consequently, Puukko[109] identified the enemies in many psalms as the Philistines (Ps 78), the Assyrians (Ps 46), the Babylonians (Ps 137), enemies of the Maccabean times (Pss 44; 74; 79; 80; 83), and so forth; and Birkeland[110] proposed that the enemies were foreign nations fighting against Israel.[111] However, such theories do not give proper consideration to individual supplications, which constitute the bigger group of psalms.

If we pay attention to the activity of the enemies as described in the psalms, it appears as very diverse and vague: they seek the life of the psalmist (Pss 35:4; 38:13), they mock him or her (Pss

31:12; 35:16), they plot against him or her (Pss 37:12; 71:10), they lay snares (Pss 31:5; 57:7), they hate and attack without cause (Pss 59:5; 69:5), they lie (Pss 109:2; 120:3). Besides, the fact that the psalmist appeals to God in order to defend his or her cause suggests that the enemy is not only against the psalmist but against God (cf. Ps 69:7–9) and all that God commands: the protection of the poor and the widow, the righteous conduct, the love of the neighbor, and the keeping of the covenant. The enemy thinks that God is far away and does not care for his people (cf. Ps 3:2; 59:7).

Therefore, the identity of the enemy in the psalms appears blurred and vague, but this allows the psalms to be applied to different situations, making their message relevant to all ages.

15. HISTORY OF THE INTERPRETATION OF THE PSALMS[112]

In ancient times, the fathers of the church interpreted the psalms with four interpretative readings: literal, allegorical, prosopological, and ethical. The *literal and historical* reading was emphasized by Theodoret (†466) and Jerome (†420). The *allegorical or symbolic* reading was stressed by Origen (180–254). The *prosopological* reading, in which each psalm is understood as spoken by a particular person (e.g., David or Christ), is found in a number of fathers. And the *ethical* reading is found in almost all fathers: their commentaries were very similar to a homily. The most outstanding commentary is the collection of homilies by Augustine, *Enarrationes in Psalmos* (AD 416).

In the Middle Ages, three main approaches were developed: *lectio divina*, which attempted to have a spiritual understanding of the psalms; the *glossa*, which attempted to identify the four senses of Scripture (literal, allegorical, moral, anagogical, or mystical);[113] and *lectio scholastica*, which gave more emphasis to the literal sense (following the order *lectio, expositio, quaestio*).

The Psalms

During and following the Renaissance, the study of ancient biblical languages and the publication of polyglots, grammars, and dictionaries gave a new impetus to the study of the psalms, giving priority to the literal or historical sense. In particular, it is worthy to mention the study of Hebrew poetry by R. Lowth (†1787).

With Hermann Gunkel (1926), there was a new beginning in the study of the psalms, discarding previous subjective readings of the psalms and looking for an objective method of study. He compared the psalms and classified them in categories, or families, according to their literary structure, vocabulary, and religious ideas.

After the contribution of Gunkel, the study of the psalms in the twentieth century has been dominated by form criticism. Accordingly, scholars attempted to identify the literary form or genre of individual psalms and to reconstruct the *Sitz im Leben* that gave birth to each literary form. In this approach, there were some developments: Sigmund Mowinckel[114] and Artur Weiser[115] emphasized above all the cultic setting of almost all psalms. Claus Westermann[116] criticized the distinction between psalms of praise and thanksgiving and attributed special relevance to the genre of supplication, considering it as the best expression of Israel's faith. Hans-Joachim Kraus[117] accepted Gunkel's view but questioned the idea that "pure" literary forms were early and "mixed" literary forms a later development; he also put additional emphasis on the theological perspective in the study of the psalms.

Erhard Gerstenberger[118] stressed the social setting of the psalms, which was relevant within small groups like the family, neighborhood, or the community, but not so much in the temple or the palace. Raymond J. Tournay[119] argued in support of a postexilic prophetic setting for many psalms. Walter Brueggemann[120] proposed to categorize the psalms in only three groups, according to their function: "psalms of orientation" (absence of tension, presence of order), "psalms of disorientation" (basically, the laments), and "psalms of reorientation" (thanksgiving and hymns). K. Seybold[121] accepted the idea that most of the psalms were composed in a cultic setting, but they began to be detached from such a setting and were readapted to new situations.

Background to Understanding the Psalms

In addition to the form citicism approach, another major contribution to the understanding of the psalms was made by the linguistic approach taken by Michael Dahood,[122] who reviewed the translation and interpretation of the psalms in the light of Northwest Semitic languages, especially Ugaritic, to the point of even excluding the vocalization of the Masoretes.

In recent times a new approach is developing, following the contribution of Gerald H. Wilson.[123] Building upon the work of Brevard Childs[124] and C. Westermann,[125] Wilson proposed to consider the psalms no longer in an isolated way, but as part of a larger framework: the five books of the Psalms.[126] In this way, each psalm is interpreted by the preceding or successive psalm, so that a "story line" or "thematic development" can be followed running from Ps 1 to Ps 150.[127] A good example of this approach is found in the two commentary volumes written by Frank Hossfeld and Eric Zenger.[128] After his work was published in 1985, Wilson refined his work,[129] speaking now of a "royal covenantal frame" and a "final wisdom frame," in which the wisdom frame takes precedence over the royal covenantal frame, so that the hope of the Israelite ultimately rests on God.

In order to distinguish this modern approach that considers the 150 psalms together, some scholars use the term *Psalter exegesis* to refer to it, as opposed to *psalms exegesis*, which refers to the analysis of individual psalms as practiced by the method of form criticism. In Psalter exegesis, the interpreter attempts to discover the place or meaning of each psalm within the whole Psalter (what can be called in German the *Sitz im Buch*, i.e., the "setting in the book"), and not the place or meaning of the psalm within its living context in ancient times (*Sitz im Leben*).

The issue of the composition and structure of the Psalms as a book is the dominant approach in modern study of the Psalms.[130] However, we have to be aware that these two approaches—studying the psalms individually or as part of the Psalter—should not be seen as mutually exclusive but as complementary.

The Psalms

16. CHRISTIAN APPROPRIATION[131]

The chief way in which the Book of Psalms differs from the other books of the Bible is that here we have not so much words, discourses, or narratives addressed to the people coming ultimately from God (laws, oracles, etc.), but the words of the people addressed to God. The Book of Psalms reveals the more active role of the people (or reader) in the individual's relationship with God. Because of this, understanding the psalms is not enough; we must also "appropriate" (i.e., "make it ours") the experience presented in the psalms. Otherwise the psalms will not be considered as what they really are: prayer.[132]

As the church receives the Book of Psalms as an inspired text and uses it in its liturgy, it is important to mention an important stage in the reading, prayer, and meditation of the psalms: the Christian believer has to appropriate the psalms, making them his or her own praise to God. The Book of Psalms is different from the other books of the OT since they present mostly feelings. We have to make ours the feelings of the psalmist, making those words our own words as we address them to God. The symbols and images used in the psalms facilitate this appropriation. The images of light and darkness, thirst and water, earth and road, freshness, solitude, dwelling, and so forth are open to be applied to our own circumstances and experiences. Only in this way will the reading and praying of the psalms become true prayer, as it is intended to be.

In order to appropriate the psalms correctly, however, we must take care to be faithful to the text of the psalms by not leaving out essential components of our spirituality: praise, thanksgiving, supplication. To sum up: we have to learn the language of the psalms.

A note can be said on the patristic method of *lectio divina*, which aimed to make the text relevant to the present situation. *Lectio divina* consists of the following main steps: 1) *lectio*: to read and understand the text; 2) *meditatio*: reflection on the lasting values of the text and its appropriation by the reader or community (what is the text saying to me or us?); and 3) *contemplatio* or *oratio*: to pass from the text to the dialogue with God and to the contemplation of God, Christ, the Spirit; it is adoration, praise, silence.[133]

17. PSALMS QUOTED IN THE NT

The Book of Psalms is the book of the Old Testament most quoted in the New Testament.[134] Most of the quotations (ca. 85 percent) come from the Septuagint (LXX). The most important quotations are from Ps 2 in reference to the resurrection of Christ and his glory as Son of God (cf. Acts 13:33; Heb 5:5); Ps 110 in reference to the dignity of Christ as Lord, and to his resurrection (Matt 22:44; 26:64; Mark 12:36; 14:62; Luke 20:42–43; 22:69; Acts 2:34–35; Heb 1:13); Ps 110 in reference to the priesthood of Christ (Heb 5:6); Ps 118 in reference to the coming of Christ as savior (Matt 21:9; 23:39; Mark 11:9–10; Luke 13:35; 19:38; John 12:13); and Ps 118 in reference to Christ being rejected and put to death, but risen by God and being the foundation of our salvation (Matt 21:9, 42; 23:39; Mark 11:9–10; 12:10–11; Luke 13:35; 19:38; 20:17; John 12:13; Acts 4:11; 1 Pet 2:7).

The fact that the NT authors have cited the texts of the psalms (as well as other texts of the OT) shows that those texts have found their fuller meaning with the coming of Christ. The psalms, and the rest of the OT, display a revelatory function that is made evident by the texts of the NT. Therefore, as it will be mentioned below, a study of the psalms cannot be limited to the mere consideration of those texts in their original context (setting in life, setting in the Psalter) but has to include their function and meaning in the entire canon of the Scriptures and in the life of the church.

The following is a list of psalm texts quoted in the New Testament:[135]

Ps 2:1–2 (LXX)	Acts 4:25–26
Ps 2:7	Acts 13:33; Heb 1:5; 5:5
Ps 4:4 (LXX)	Eph 4:26

The Psalms

Ps 5:9 (LXX)	Rom 3:13
Ps 8:3 (LXX)	Matt 21:16
Ps 8:4–6 (LXX)	Heb 2:6–8
Ps 8:6	1 Cor 15:27
Ps 10:7 (LXX)	Rom 3:14
Ps 14:1–8	Rom 3:10–12
Ps 16:8–11 (LXX)	Acts 2:25–28
Ps 16:10	Acts 2:31
Ps 16:10 (LXX)	Acts 13:35
Ps 18:49	Rom 15:9
Ps 19:4 (LXX)	Rom 10:18
Ps 22:1	Matt 27:46; Mark 15:34
Ps 22:18	John 19:24
Ps 22:22	Heb 2:12
Ps 24:1	1 Cor 10:26
Ps 31:5	Luke 23:46
Ps 32:1–2	Rom 4:7–8
Ps 34:12–16	1 Pet 3:10–12
Ps 35:19	John 15:25
Ps 36:1	Rom 3:18
Ps 40:6–8	Heb 10:5–7
Ps 41:9	John 13:18
Ps 44:22	Rom 8:36
Ps 45:6–7	Heb 1:8–9
Ps 51:4 (LXX)	Rom 3:4
Ps 53:1–3	Rom 3:10–12
Ps 68:18	Eph 4:8
Ps 69:4	John 15:25
Ps 69:9	John 2:17; Rom 15:3
Ps 69:22–23 (LXX)	Rom 11:9–10
Ps 69:25	Acts 1:20
Ps 78:2	Matt 13:35
Ps 78:24	John 6:31
Ps 82:6	John 10:34
Ps 89:20	Acts 13:22
Ps 91:11–12	Matt 4:6; Luke 4:10–11
Ps 94:11	1 Cor 3:20
Ps 95:7–8 (LXX)	Heb 3:15; 4:7

Background to Understanding the Psalms

Ps 95:7-11	Heb 3:7-11
Ps 95:11	Heb 4:3, 5
Ps 102:25-27 (LXX)	Heb 1:10-12
Ps 104:4 (LXX)	Heb 1:7
Ps 109:8	Acts 1:20
Ps 110:1	Matt 22:44; 26:64; Mark 12:36; 14:62; Luke 20:42-43; 22:69; Acts 2:34-35; Heb 1:13
Ps 110:4	Heb 5:6; 7:17, 21
Ps 112:9	2 Cor 9:9
Ps 116:10 (LXX)	2 Cor 4:13
Ps 117:1	Rom 15:11
Ps 118:6 (LXX)	Heb 13:6
Ps 118:22	Luke 20:17; Acts 4;11; 1 Pet 2:7
Ps 118:22-23	Matt 21:42; Mark 12:10-11
Ps 118:25-26	Matt 21:9; Mark 11:9-10; John 12:13
Ps 118:26	Matt 23:39; Luke 13:35; 19:38
Ps 132:11	Acts 2:30
Ps 140:3 (LXX)	Rom 3:13

18. STUDYING THE PSALMS

Finally, I offer some practical advice for a methodological study of the psalms, taking into account the contribution of modern exegesis.

1. *An attentive reading.* The first thing to do is to read the psalm attentively, trying *to understand* the meaning of the text, the feelings presented by the intended author and communicated to the reader, and to identify a line of thought that runs throughout the psalm.
2. *Literary analysis.* Once this is done, the next step is to identify the *literary genre* of the psalm and to recognize the *literary structure* of the psalm, indicating the main parts of the text. For this purpose, part 2 of this book presents a brief description of the most important literary forms

used in the psalms, with their main characteristics and their basic literary structure. In addition, try to determine the situation of the psalmist as portrayed in the psalm: Is the psalmist speaking alone or as representative of the community? Is he or she speaking on behalf of himself or herself or of someone else? Is he or she in affliction or at peace? Does the psalmist pray at home? At the temple? Who speaks in the psalm? The king? A sick person? A priest? The people of Israel?

3. *Historical analysis.* The next step is to try to identify the concrete historical setting of the psalm, the situation of the real author of the psalm, and a possible date of composition. Was the psalm composed for a liturgical celebration at the temple? For a ceremony at the king's palace? For an individual at home facing difficulties? Was it composed before or after the exile? Since the language of the psalm is often vague, it is difficult to determine the historical situation that gave birth to the text. Moreover, one has to be aware that the text most probably went through an adaptation and reworking at a later time, and this complicates the historical analysis. However, any clue that can be grasped will be helpful for the analysis in the next step.

4. *Theological analysis.* Once we have familiarized ourselves sufficiently with the literary and historical aspects of the psalm, it is time to examine the theological ideas communicated in the text. What is the main theological idea developed through the psalm? Can one verse be chosen that summarizes the entire psalm? In order to give a correct answer, it is necessary to pay attention to the literary genre of the psalm. What secondary theological ideas are expressed in the psalm? What is the theological view offered regarding salvation, God, the human person, or the community? Is it possible to relate the message of this psalm to the preceding or successive psalms?

5. *Christian appropriation.* The last step in our study of the psalm is the appropriation of the psalm, so that the words of the text become ours and the psalm becomes relevant to our present situation. The preceding literary, historical,

and theological analysis will assist us in this task, so that our appropriation does not become a manipulation, forcing the text to say what we want and not allowing the text to speak by itself. This appropriation can take place at the personal level (prayer and meditation) and at the community level (pastoral application).

With these steps in mind, it is suggested that, after reading this introduction, you try to study a psalm of your choice from each of the eleven different categories of psalms following the steps suggested here, and making use of at least one or two commentaries (see the bibliography at the end of this book). If you study the psalms within a group, a good exercise would be to share your own study with the other members of the class or study group.

NOTES

1. For introductions on the Psalms see the introduction to each of the commentaries listed in the bibliography at the end of this book. Good examples are David FIRTH and Philip JOHNSTON, eds., *Interpreting the Psalms: Issues and Approaches* (Downers Grove, IL: InterVarsity Press, 2005); Hans-Joachim KRAUS, *Psalms 1—59. A Commentary* (Minneapolis: Augsburg Fortress Press, 1988), 11–111; P. C. CRAIGIE, *Psalms*, WBC 19 (Waco, TX: Word Books, 1983), 25–56; Leopold SABOURIN, *The Psalms: Their Origin and Meaning* (New York: Alba House, 1974).

2. This is the *Psalterium Gallicanum*, prepared by Jerome in AD 386 in Bethlehem, which is a revision of the LXX in the light of the Hexapla. But later he produced the *Psalterium juxta Hebraeos*, a direct translation from the Hebrew text. The *Liber Psalmorum*, published in 1969 as part of the *Nova Vulgata*, was a revision of the *Psalterium Gallicanum*, corrected by the text of the Hebrew psalter (MT) when necessary. On the other hand, the *Psalterium Romanum* seems to be the text of the *Vetus Latina* (Old Latin translation of the Bible).

3. The psalms are numbered in the Greek manuscripts; but in the Hebrew manuscripts the earliest evidence for this is in the medieval period.

4. *Nova vulgata bibliorum sacrorum editio* (Vatican City: Libreria editrice Vaticana, 1979).

5. K. Elliger and W. Rudolph, eds., *Biblia hebraica stuttgartensia* (Stuttgart: Deutsche Bibelstiftung, 1967–77); R. Kittel, ed., *Biblia hebraica* (Württemburg: Württembergische Bibelanstalt, 1954).

6. Kraus, *Psalms 1—59*, 16–17. This division was already acknowledged by some of the fathers of the church, who noted that the first, second, and third books end with "Amen, Amen," the fourth with "Amen, Hallelujah," and the fifth with "Hallelujah."

7. *Midrash Tehillim* Ps 1:1: "Moses gave Israel the Five Books, and David gave Israel the five books of Psalms."

8. So, for example, Jerome: "Five sections and one volume of the psalms" (PL 29:599; cf. also PL 28:1183).

9. G. H. Wilson, "The Structure of the Psalter," in Firth and Johnston, *Interpreting the Psalms*, 235.

10. See the section below on "History of the Interpretation of the Psalms."

11. Wilson, "Structure," 236.

12. W. Brueggemann, "Bounded by Obedience and Praise: The Psalms as Canon," *JSOT* 50 (1991): 63–92. See also Patrick D. Miller, "Psalm 73 as a Canonical Marker," *JSOT* 72 (1996): 45–56.

13. C. Westermann, *Praise and Lament in the Psalms* (Atlanta: John Knox Press, 1981), 257.

14. Wilson, "Structure," 238.

15. On this attribution, see James Luther Mays, "The David of the Psalms," *Int* 40 (1986): 143–55.

16. On these psalms, see Michael Goulder, *The Psalms of the Sons of Korah*, JSOTSS 20, (Sheffield Academic Press, 1983).

17. If we consider the first collection of Pss 1—41 as "of David," then this collection would be the "Second Collection of Psalms of David."

18. The Hebrew word הלל "Hallel" means "praise." The first "Hallel" (known also as the "Hallel of Egypt" or "Lesser Hallel") is recited or sung during the Passover meal (Pss 113—114 were recited before the meal, and Pss 115—118 after the meal; cf. Matt 26:30; Mark 14:26), as well as on other feasts (on the first day of the Feast of Unleavened Bread, on Pentecost, and on the Feast of Booths); the second one (known also as the "Great Hallel") concludes the Passover meal and the prayer at the synagogue on Sabbath; the third one belongs to the postexilic liturgy.

19. That is, poetic variants of Deut 26:5–9 and Josh 24:1–13.

20. On the titles of the psalms, see Elieser Slomovic, "Toward an Understanding of the Formation of the Historical Titles in the Book of Psalms," *ZAW* 91 (1979): 350–80; Brevard S. Childs, "Psalms Titles and Midrashic Exegesis," *JSS* 16 (1971): 137–50; J. Enciso, "Los títulos de los

Salmos y la historia de la formación del salterio," *EstBib* 13 (1954): 135–66. For a basic explanation of some titles, see Nancy L. deClaissé-Walford, *Introduction to the Psalms: A Song from Ancient Israel* (St. Louis: Chalice Press, 2004), 151–55.

21. See, for example, Pss 3:3, 5, 9; 4:3, 5. On the meaning of *selah*, see Norman H. Snaith, "Selah," *VT* 2 (1952): 43–56.

22. Craigie, *Psalms*, 76–77; Kraus, *Psalms 1—59*, 27–29.

23. The attribution is made through the use of the Hebrew preposition *lamed*: ל, *le*, which has been interpreted traditionally with the meaning of authorship: "Psalm of David" = "Psalm composed by David." But the situation is not clear. The basic meaning of the preposition *le* is simply "to." Besides, from a comparison with the Ugaritic, the preposition seems to indicate only a generic relationship, including the meaning "concerning" or "about." On this issue, see H. Cazelles, "La question du 'lamed auctoris,'" *RB* 56 (1949): 93–101; G. Castellino, *Libro dei Salmi*, La Sacra Bibbia (Roma-Torino: Marietti, 1955), 16.

24. Asaph was David's chief musician (1 Chr 16:5–6) and the group of Levites belonging to him were also musicians (2 Chr 5:12). Most probably, the title "A Psalm of Asaph" given to some psalms indicates that the psalm belonged to the collection of this guild. On these psalms, see Harry Nasuti, *Tradition History and the Psalms of Asaph*, SBLDS 88 (Atlanta: SBL Press, 1988).

25. The descendants of Korah were one of the Levite choirs (2 Chr 20:19), together with the Kohathites. On the Korahites, see G. Wanke, *Die Zionstheologie der Korachiten in ihrem traditionsgeschichtlichen Zusammenhang*, BZAW 97 (Berlin: De Gruyter, 1966).

26. Gerald H. Wilson, *The Editing of the Hebrew Psalter*, SBLDS 76 (Chico, CA: SBL Press, 1985, 2004).

27. H. Gunkel, *Die Psalmen*, HKAT (Göttingen: Vandenhoeck & Ruprecht, 1926, 1968); Engl. transl.: *The Psalms: A Form-Critical Introduction*, trans. Thomas M. Horner (Philadelphia: Fortress Press, 1967). This magnum opus by Gunkel was unfortunately left unfinished. His pupil Joachim Begrich put the final touches on the organization of Gunkel's last work on the psalms, and it was published in 1933 as H. Gunkel and J. Begrich, *Einleitung in die Psalmen: Die Gattungen der religiosen Lyrik Israels* (Göttingen: Vandenhoeck & Ruprecht, 1933, 1966); Engl. transl.: *Introduction to the Psalms: The Genres of the Religious Lyric of Israel*, trans. James D. Nogalski (Macon, GA: Mercer University Press, 1998).

The Psalms

28. By Castellino, *Salmi*, who uses several criteria for his classification, giving great importance to the opening lines of the psalm, what he calls "the criterion of the beginning."

29. The psalm is written as acrostic, in which successive verses begin with successive letters of the alphabet.

30. Mitchell First, "Can Archeology Help Date the Psalms?" *BAR* 38 (2012): 53–56. First notices that the Book of Lamentations (chap. 2, 3, 4), written between 586 and 538 BC, also follows the order *pê-'ayin* in its acrostics.

31. So the common designation of the Psalter as "Hymnbook of the Second Temple."

32. For some classic and recent works on the theme, see Jens Kamlah and Henrike Michelau, *Temple Building and Temple Cult: Architecture and Cultic Paraphernalia of Temples in the Levant (2.–1. Mill. B.C.E.). Proceedings of a Conference on the Occasion of the 50th Anniversary of the Institute of Biblical Archaeology at the University of Tübingen (28–30 May 2010)* (Wiesbaden: Harrassowitz, 2012); Reinhard Gregor Kratz and Hermann Spieckermann, *One God–One Cult–One Nation: Archaeological and Biblical Perspectives*, BZAW 405 (Berlin: De Gruyter, 2010); John Day, *Temple and Worship in Biblical Israel*, proceedings of the Oxford Old Testament Seminar (London: T & T Clark, 2005); Gerald A. Klingbeil, "Altars, Ritual and Theology—Preliminary Thoughts on the Importance of Cult and Ritual for a Theology of the Hebrew Scriptures," *VT* 54 (2004): 495–515; R. H. Lowery, *The Reforming Kings: Cults and Society in First Temple Judah* (Sheffield: Academic Press, 1991); Peter Dubovsky, *The Temple in Ancient Israel* (forthcoming); Erhard S. Gerstenberger, *Psalms. Part I with an Introduction to Cultic Poetry* (Grand Rapids: Eerdmans, 1988).

33. R. de Vaux, *Institutions de l'ancien testament* (Paris: Cerf, 1961), 145. Eng. translation: *Ancient Israel: Its Life and Institutions*, trans. John McHugh, vol. 1 (New York: McGraw Hill, 1961), 145.

34. In comparison to other temples of that time, the Solomonic Temple was a small temple: the temple at Luxor in Egypt, built by Amenophis III (1412–1375 BC), was 190 m. long and 55 m. wide; in Babylon, the temple Esagila was about 80 m. x 83 m. (cf. M. de Tuya and J. Salguero, *Introducción a la Biblia*, BAC 268, vol. 2 [Madrid: BAC, 1967], 442).

35. 1 Kgs 6:20–21; 7:48–50.

36. Exod 26:33. It is this veil that it is referred to by the evangelists: Matt 27:51; Mark 15:38; Luke 23:45.

37. The title of Ps 29 in the Hebrew reads only, "Psalm of David," but the Greek reads, "Psalm of David. At the end of the Feast of Tabernacles."

38. In reference to the Talmud, it has been suggested that Pss 120—134 ("Psalms of Ascents") be considered as fifteen psalms recited during the first day of the Feast of Tabernacles by the Levites standing on the fifteen steps leading to the court of the temple. But the Talmud (*Middot*, 2.5; cf. *Sukka* 51b) only makes a comparison between the fifteen steps and the fifteen psalms, without saying that they were sung by the Levites for that occasion (cf. CASTELLINO, *Salmi*, 14; Franz DELITZSCH, *Biblischer Kommentar über die Psalmen* [Leipzig: Dörffling und Franke, 1883], 780).

39. So Briggs, Kirkpatrick, Kittel, Gunkel.

40. Probably also Ps 135.

41. Psalms that celebrate the Exodus (e.g., Pss 105; 114; 135—136; 147) could have been sung during the feast (Richard J. CLIFFORD, *Psalms 1—72*, AOTC [Nashville, TX: Abingdon, 2002], 19).

42. Psalms 50 and 81 would have been appropriate to this feast since they urge for the observance of the covenant and the Law given at Sinai (CLIFFORD, *Psalms 1—72*, 19-20).

43. D. R. AP-THOMAS, "Notes on Some Terms Relating to Prayer," *VT* 6 (1956): 225-41.

44. After the reform of Josiah that centralized the cult in the temple of Jerusalem, only the Levites, descendants of the family of Zadok, were allowed to serve as priests in the temple (see Ezek 40:46; 43:19; 44:15; 48:11; Num 18:1, 6-7).

45. G. WIGODER, ed., "Temple" in *The Encyclopedia of Judaism* (Jerusalem: The Jerusalem Publishing House, 1989), 695.

46. *Arakhin* 2, 3-3.

47. The date of Ezra's mission to Jerusalem is debated: some scholars put it in 458 BC. But A. VON HOONACKER (*Néhémie et Esdras: Nouvelle hypothèse sur la chronologie de l'époque de la Restauration juive* [Louvain: Istas, 1890]) proposed the date of 398 BC. This latter date seems preferable (see H. G. M WILLIAMSON, *Ezra, Nehemiah*, WBC 16 [Waco, TX: Word Books, 1985]).

48. According to rabbinic tradition, Ezra established the Great Assembly (Sanhedrin), and ordained the reading of the law at the Sabbath afternoon service and at Monday and Thursday morning services. He also changed the script from the ancient Hebrew script to the Assyrian square script.

49. See also Pss 91; 94; 104.

50. WILSON, "Structure," 241.

The Psalms

51. These are Pss 1; 3; 4; 20; 21; 32; 41; 46; 55; 58; 61; 64; 65; 70; 72—75; 80; 87.

52. The best example to show the differences is Ps 145; cf. André PAUL, *La Bible avant la Bible. La grande révélation des manuscrits de la mer Morte* (Paris: Cerf, 2005), 123-25.

53. J. A. SANDERS, *The Psalms Scroll of Qumran Cave 11 (11QPs^a)*, DJD 4 (Oxford: Oxford University Press, 1965).

54. The identification of some psalms is dubious. The titles in italics refer to noncanonical texts.

55. The two small scrolls of psalms discovered at Masada: MasPs^a (Pss 81:2—85:6) and MasPs^b (Pss 147—150), follow the order of the psalms in the Hebrew Bible.

56. "The presence of these other Psalms or compositions in some of the Psalms scrolls alerts us to the fact that the 'Book of Psalms' at Qumran should not automatically be equated with the Psalter that appears in our Bibles." M. ABEGG Jr., P. FLINT, and E. ULRICH, *The Dead Sea Scrolls Bible* (New York: Harper Collins, 1999), 506.

57. WILSON, "Structure," 242-43; see also G. H. WILSON, "The Qumran Psalms Scroll (11QPs^a) and the Canonical Psalter: Comparison of Editorial Shapping," *CBQ* 59 (1997): 448-64.

58. This pesher considers Ps 1:1 and Ps 2:1 together with parts of 2 Sam 7:10-14; Exod 15:17-18; Amos 9:11; Isa 8:11; Ezek 37:23(?); Dan 12:10; 11:32; Deut 33:8-11, 19-21. This commentary presents the idea of the restoration of the temple, the coming of the descendant of David, and the teaching of the law.

59. J. H. CHARLESWORTH, ed., *The Old Testament Pseudepigrapha*, vol. 2, AB (New York: Doubleday, 1985), 609-771.

60. J. A. SANDERS, "Cave 11 Surprises and the Question of the Canon," in *New Directions in Biblical Archeology*, ed. D. N. Freedman and J. C. Greenfield, 113-30 (New York: Doubleday, 1971). See also J. MAGNE, "Recherches sur les Psaumes 151, 154 et 15," *RQ* 8 (1975): 503-7.

61. H. E. RYLE and M. R. JAMES, *Psalms of the Pharisees: Commonly Called the Psalms of Solomon* (Cambridge: Cambridge University Press, 1891).

62. So A. DUPONT-SOMMER, *The Essene Writings from Qumran* (New York: World Pub. Co., 1962), 296; Otto EISSFELDT, *The Old Testament: An Introduction* (New York: Harper & Row, 1965), 610-13.

63. Kenton L. SPARKS, *Ancient Texts for the Study of the Hebrew Bible: A Guide to the Background Literature* (Peabody, MA: Hendrickson, 2005), 84-126; Klaus SEYBOLD, *Introducing the Psalms* (Edinburgh: T & T Clark,

1990), 191–212; C. L. Feinberg, "Parallels to the Psalms in Near Eastern Literature," *BibSacra* 104 (1947): 290–97.

64. For the text, see Pritchard, *ANET*, 104–6. On the Canaanite background of Ps 29, see H. Strauss, "Zur Auslegung von Ps 29 auf dem Hintergrund seiner kanaanäischen Bezüge," *ZAW* 82 (1970): 91–102; Cf. also Seybold, *Introducing*, 201–2.

65. For the text, see *ANET*, 370; V. C. Matthews and D. C. Benjamin, eds., *Old Testament Parallels: Laws and Stories from the Ancient Near East* (Mahwah, NJ: Paulist Press, 1997), 257–61; cf. also Seybold, *Introducing*, 203–7.

66. Gaster thinks that the psalmist of Ps 29 took a Canaanite psalm and only substituted the name of Baal with the name of Yahweh (T. H. Gaster, "Psalm 29," *JQR* 37 [1946–47]: 55–65).

67. H. Cazelles, "Une relecture du Psaume 29?," in *A la rencontre de Dieu. Mémorial Albert Gelin*, ed. A. Barucq et al, 119–28 (Le Puy: Editions Xavier Mappus, 1961). Cited by Sabourin, *Psalms*, 181.

68. Castellino, *Salmi*, 456.

69. G. Nagel, "A propos des rapports du Psaume 104 avec les textes egyptiens," *FS für A. Bertholet* (Tübingen: JCB Mohr, 1950), 395–403; cited by Sabourin, *Psalms*, 185.

70. So Sparks, *Ancient*, 117.

71. Ibid., 118. Castellino (*Salmi*, 184) indicates two different interpretations on this psalm: the "personal interpretation" (Gunkel) and the "national interpretation" (Birkeland, Buttenweiser). Those who adopt the personal interpretation tend to consider the last verses as a postexilic addition.

72. Sparks, *Ancient*, 118.

73. Ibid.

74. Ibid., 119.

75. On the subject, see W. G. E. Watson, *Classical Hebrew Poetry: A Guide to Its Techniques*, JSOTSS 26 (Sheffield: Sheffield Academic Press, 1984).

76. Robert Lowth, *De Sacra Poesie Hebraeorum Praelectiones Academicae* (Oxford, 1753).

77. It was first pointed out by A. S. Mazzocchi (1684–1771), but received its name from R. Lowth. On the subject, see A. Berlin, *The Dynamics of Biblical Parallelism* (Bloomington, IN: Indiana University Press, 1985); J. L. Kugel, *The Idea of Biblical Poetry: Parallelism and Its History* (New Haven: Yale University Press, 1981); S. A. Geller, *Parallelism in Early Biblical Poetry*, HSM 20 (Missoula, MT: Scholars Press, 1979).

78. Cf. also vv. 2–6.

The Psalms

79. This example is taken from Alastair G. Hunter, *An Introduction to the Psalms*, T & T Clark Approaches to Biblical Studies (London: T & T Clark, 2008), 15. Another example is Ps 29:10.

80. Cf. also vv. 8–9.

81. Example taken from Hunter, *Psalms*, 15.

82. This example is given by J. L. McKenzie, "Poetry," in *Dictionary of the Bible* (New York: The Bruce Pub. Co., 1965), 680.

83. Nowadays, this kind of figure is not as commonly used as in ancient times; however, we have some examples of it. So the phrase attributed to Winston Churchill: "We make a living by what we get, we make a life by what we give" (some attribute it to Norman MacEwen).

84. On the subject, see M. O'Connor, *Hebrew Verse Structure* (Winona Lake, IN: Eisenbrauns, 1980).

85. On this, see S. Mowinckel, *The Psalms in Israel's Worship*, vol. 2 (Nashville: Blackwell, 1962), 162.

86. Examples taken from Wilfrid Harrington, *Record of the Promise: The Old Testament* (Chicago: The Priory Press, 1965), 282; the Bible passages are taken from the RSV and ESV, respectively.

87. This feature is not present in modern translations of the psalm.

88. For example, the repetition of the words "Yahweh is King!" in Ps 96:10 and Ps 97:1. On this figure, see W. Zimmerli, "Zwillingpsalmen," *Wort, Lied und Gottesspruch. FS J. Ziegler*, ed. J. Schreiner, 105–13 (Stuttgart: Verlag Katholisches Bibelwerk, 1972). Zimmerli identifies as pairs the following psalms using the *concatenatio*: Pss 1—2; 3—4; 9—10; 30—31; 31—32; 32—33; 38—39; 40—41; 43—44; 69—70; 73—74; 74—75; 77—78; 79—80; 80—81; 105—106; 111—112; 127—128.

89. Ps 122:7-8: "Peace (*shalom*) within your walls…peace (*shalom*) upon you" (my translation); see also Ps 8:2, 10.

90. So for example, the repetition of the word אשרי, *'ashrê* "happy" in Ps 1:1 and Ps 41:1, delimitating the first book of psalms; or in Ps 1:1 and Ps 2:12, considering both psalms as a unit.

91. Ps 96:4b–5a: "More awesome than any of the gods (*'elōhîm*), all the gods of the nations are idols (*'elîlîm*)," my translation.

92. Isa 14:22d: "Offspring (*nîn*) and posterity (*neked*) declares (*ne'um*) Yahweh," my translation.

93. Ps 122:6a: "Pray (*sha'ălû*) for the peace (*shelôm*) of Jerusalem (*Yerûshâlaîm*)."

94. On this, the aphorism of L. Alonso-Schökel is relevant: "What was written with imagination, has to be read with imagination."

95. On the general problems of understanding biblical Hebrew and related languages, see S. Moscati, ed., *An Introduction to the Comparative Grammar of the Semitic Languages* (Wiesbaden: Otto Harrasowitz, 1964).

96. Craigie, *Psalms*, 110.

97. The waw-conversive or waw-consecutive is a grammatical construction in classical Hebrew that consists of prefixing a verb with the letter *waw*. This addition affects the tense or aspect of the verb.

98. So, following the theory of Paul Joüon, *Grammaire de l'hébreu biblique*, 2nd ed. (Rome: Biblical Institute Press, 1947).

99. Castellino follows the reading of the LXX and Vg and considers Ps 4 as a thanksgiving psalm: the psalmist mentions a salvific act of God and gives thanks. Also, Gunkel interprets the verbal form as a past tense, "answered me," in order to agree with the following phrase in v. 1: "You gave me room when I was in distress." However, most scholars prefer to adopt the reading of the Masoretes, understanding an imperative: "Answer me."

100. Castellino, *Salmi*, 25–29. See also H. J. Kraus, *Theologie der Psalmen* (Neukirchen-Vluyn: Neukirchener Verlag, 1979); Eng. translation: *Theology of the Psalms*, trans. Keith Crim (Minneapolis: Fortress Press, 1992); Tiziano Lorenzin, *I Salmi*, I Libri Biblici 20 (Milano: Paoline, 2001), 545–66.

101. On this, we follow mainly Sabourin, *Psalms*, 95–104.

102. Lorenzin, *Salmi*, 565.

103. It has been debated whether the words *'ānî* and *'ānāw* refer to the same people or not (a social condition for the former, and a religious condition for the latter); on the history of the debate, see P. van den Berghe, "*'ānî* et *'ānāw* dans les Psaumes," in *Le Psautier*, ed. R. De Langhe (Louvain: Orientalia et Biblica Loveneinsia IV, 1962), 273–95; cited by Sabourin, *Psalms*, 95.

104. So the frequent combination of the words עני ואביון, *'ānî w'ebyôn* (Pss 37:14; 40:17; 70:5; 74:21).

105. Rudolf Kittel, *Die Psalmen*, KAT 13 (Leipzig: Deichertsche Verlagsbuchhandlung, 1929); A. Gelin, *Les Pauvres de Yahvé* (Paris: Cerf, 1953).

106. Gelin, *Pauvres*, 28.

107. So for example, Sabourin notices that in Ps 34, the psalmist uses the words *poor, just one*, and *saint* referring to the same people: "poor" (34:3,7), "saints" (34:10), "just" (34:16, 20, 22) (Sabourin, *Psalms*, 99).

108. On this, we follow Sabourin, *Psalms*, 114–17.

109. A. Puukko, "Der Feind in den Alttestamentlichen Psalmen," *OTS* 7 (1950): 47–65.

110. H. BIRKELAND, *The Evildoers in the Book of Psalms* (Oslo: Kommisjon Hos Jacob Dybwad, 1955).

111. This theory has been criticized by M. TSEVAT, *A Study of the Language of the Biblical Psalms*, JBLMS 9 (Philadelphia: SBL Press, 1965).

112. S. GILLINGHAM, *Psalms through the Centuries*, vol. 1 (Oxford: Wiley-Blackwell, 2008); David M. HOWARD, "The Psalms and Current Study," in FIRTH AND JOHNSTON, *Interpreting the Psalms*, 23–40; LORENZIN, *Salmi*, 570–80; CRAIGIE, *Psalms*, 43–48; J. Kenneth KUNTZ, "Engaging the Psalms: Gains and Trends in Recent Research," *CRBS* 2 (1994): 77–106; W. L. HOLLADAY, *The Psalms through Three Thousand Years: Prayerbook of a Cloud of Witnesses* (Minneapolis: Fortress Press, 1993).

113. H. BOESE, "Die alte 'glossa psalmorum ex traditione seniorum,'" *Vetus Latina* 9 (1982): 35. This glossa was based mainly on the work of Augustine, Jerome, and Gregory. As an example of these four senses, one can consider Ps 122, which tells of the joy of the Jewish people as they approached Jerusalem, containing all four of these aspects: Jerusalem is a city that they travel to (literal sense), any place where pilgrims gather together for internal cleansing and prayer to God, as for example the church (allegorical sense), our soul where we pray to God (moral sense), and heaven (mystical sense).

114. MOWINCKEL, *Psalms*, 12.

115. Artur WEISER, *Die Psalmen* (Göttingen: Vandenhoeck & Ruprecht, 1955); Eng. translation: *The Psalms: A Commentary*, trans. Herbert Hartwell, OTL (Philadelphia: Westminster John Knox Press, 1962).

116. C. WESTERMANN, *Praise and Lament in the Psalms* (Atlanta: John Knox Press, 1981); C. WESTERMANN, *The Living Psalms* (Grand Rapids: Eerdmans, 1989).

117. H. J. KRAUS, *Psalms. A Commentary*, 2 vols. (Minneapolis: Fortress Press, 1988–89); *Theology of the Psalms*.

118. E. S. GERSTENBERGER, *Psalms*, part 1, FOTL 14 (Grand Rapids: Eerdmans, 1988); part 2, FOTL 15 (Grand Rapids: Eerdmans, 2001).

119. Raymond J. TOURNAY, *Seeing and Hearing God in the Psalms: The Prophetic Liturgy of the Second Temple in Jerusalem*, JSOTSS 118 (Sheffield: JSOT Press, 1991).

120. W. BRUEGGEMANN, *The Message of the Psalms: A Theological Commentary* (Minneapolis: Augsburg, 1984).

121. K. SEYBOLD, *Die Psalmen*, HAT 1/15 (Tübingen: Mohr-Siebeck, 1996).

122. M. DAHOOD, *Psalms*, 3 vols, AB 16–17A (Garden City–New York: Doubleday, 1966–70). See also M. DAHOOD and T. PENAR, "The Grammar of the Psalter," in ibid., 3:361–456).

123. Gerald H. WILSON, *The Editing of the Hebrew Psalter*, SBLDS 76 (Chico, CA: Scholars Press, 1985, 2004). However, GREGORY of Nyssa (†394), in his *Explanation of the Titles of the Psalms*, already proposed to consider the first psalm of each of the five books of the Psalms as the interpretive key for the whole book (Cf. LORENZIN, *Salmi*, 571).

124. Brevard S. CHILDS, *An Introduction to the Old Testament as Scripture* (Philadelphia: Fortress Press, 1979).

125. WESTERMANN, *Praise and Lament in the Psalms*.

126. See, for example, Gianni BARBIERO, *Das erste Psalmenbuch als Einheit. Eine synchrone Analyse von Psalm 1—41*, OBS 16 (New York: Peter Lang, 1999); E. ZENGER, "The Composition and Theology of the Fifth Book of the Psalms, Ps 107—145," *JSOT* 80 (1998): 77-102.

127. For an introduction considering this approach, see E. ZENGER, "The Psalter as a Book: Observations about Its Origin, Composition and Function," in *The Psalms in Recent Research*, ed. P. D. Miller and D. M. Howard, SBTS (Winona Lake, IN: Eisenbrauns, forthcoming); original German available in E. ZENGER, ed., *Der Psalter in Judentum und Christentum*, HBS 18 (Freiburg: Herder, 1998), 1-57; J. C. MCCANN, *A Theological Introduction to the Book of Psalms: The Psalms as a Torah* (Nashville: Abingdon Press, 1993); P. D. MILLER, *Interpreting the Psalms* (Philadelphia: Fortress Press, 1986). For a criticism against this approach, see N. WHYBRAY, *Reading the Psalms as a Book*, JSOTSS 222 (Sheffield: Sheffield Academic Press, 1996).

128. Frank Lothar HOSSFELD and Erich ZENGER, *Psalms 2*, Hermeneia (Minneapolis, MN: Fortress Press, 2005); this volume covers Pss 51—100; F. L. HOSSFELD and E. ZENGER, *Psalms 3*, Hermeneia (Minneapolis, MN: Fortress Press, 2011); this volume covers Pss 101—150. In Italian, see LORENZIN, *Salmi*.

129. G. H. WILSON, "The Shape of the Book of Psalms," *Int* 46 (1992): 129-42; G. H. WILSON, "Shaping the Psalter: A Consideration of Editorial Linkage in the Book of Psalms," in *The Shape and Shaping of the Psalter*, ed. J. C. McCann, 72-82, JSOTSS 159 (Sheffield: Sheffield Academic Press, 1993); WILSON, "Structure," 229-46.

130. See R. Dean ANDERSON, "The Division and Order of the Psalms," *WTJ* 56 (1994): 219-41; Gerald H. WILSON, "Evidence of Editorial Divisions in the Hebrew Psalter," *VT* 34 (1984): 337-52.

131. This Christian appropriation is one of the contributions of Luis ALONSO-SCHÖKEL and Cecilia CARNITI, *I Salmi*, Commenti Biblici, 2 vols (Rome: Borla, 1992-93); the section on the Christian appropriation was written by ALONSO-SCHÖKEL.

132. L. Alonso-Schökel, *Treinta Salmos: Poesía y Oración* (Madrid: Ediciones Cristiandad, 1986), 26.

133. This classical division into *memory, intellect, will* is very old and was developed especially by Augustine. A more detailed explanation of the *lectio divina* involves the following progressive steps: 1) *lectio*; 2) *meditatio*; 3) *oratio* ("Lord, make me understand the permanent values I am missing in the text"); 4) *contemplatio*; 5) *consolatio* (gift of the Spirit: joy, peace..., not obligatory, is a gift) (this is the atmosphere proper to great interior choices); 6) *discretio* (we become sensitive to all that is gospel and all that is not); 7) *deliberatio* (we learn to discern and decide); 8) *actio* (action moved by prayer; we do not read Scripture to have strength to carry out what we have decided, but we read and meditate to understand what to do).

134. The quotations from the Psalms constitute about one-third of all OT quotations in the NT. On the use of the Psalms in the NT, see S. B. Frost, "The Christian Interpretation of the Psalms," *CJT* 5 (1959): 25–34.

135. Taken from *The Greek New Testament*, 3rd ed (New York: UBS, 1975), 897–98.

PART II

Categories of Psalms[1]

1. INDIVIDUAL SUPPLICATIONS[2]

The individual psalms of supplication present a suffering humanity that, in its distress and having apparently been forgotten by God, appeals to God. About 40 percent of the psalms are in this category. They usually present three groups of characters: the psalmist, God, and the enemies.[3] Their basic structure is the following:

1. *Opening Appeal*: This is the introductory part of the psalm, which can present different forms: "My God" (Ps 22:2), "I said to Yahweh, 'You are my God'" (Pss 140:7; 31:15; translation altered).
2. *Exposition of the Case*: The suppliant presents to God his or her situation of anguish, need, sickness, or persecution. The phrases "Why?" or "How long?" are characteristic of this part. The presentation of the case can be very short (Ps 54:5). Usually this part is introduced by the Hebrew word כִּי *kî* ("because," "since"), which provides the reason for the supplication.
3. *Supplication*: Here we have the characteristic vocabulary of these psalms: "Hear me," "give ear to my words," "listen to my cry," "your face do not turn away from me," "awake, my God," "up," "come quickly," "do not delay," "save me," and so on. Sometimes the appeal for the forgiveness of sins is also mentioned. Notable is the imprecation against the enemies (Pss 69:23–29; 70:3–4; 109:6–20; 137:9).[4] The suppliant appeals to the mercy, the fidelity, the righteousness of God, and bases his or her supplication on his or her confidence and human weakness, which needs God's help. Since God is a righteous God, God will protect those who seek to live in a righteous way and punish the evildoers.
4. *Certainty of Being Heard and Thanksgiving*: Usually the psalm concludes with the certainty that God has listened

to the supplication. The psalmist anticipates the future and sees himself or herself in the act of fulfilling his or her vow of thanksgiving in the temple through a sacrifice (cf. Pss 22:24–25; 54:8–9) or singing a song of gratitude.

The attention of scholars has been directed to the unexpected change in these psalms from the moment of supplication to that of joyful thanksgiving. Several explanations have been proposed:[5] a) the thanksgiving represents only the certainty that one is being heard, and the vow of thanksgiving; b) the thanksgiving part is to be emphasized over the supplication, so that these psalms are in reality "thanksgiving psalms"; c) the supplication and the thanksgiving are two prayers, with different *Sitz im Leben*, that were put together later; and d) between the supplication and the thanksgiving, we have to suppose a salvific event (an oracle by the priest, a cultic theophany in a feast of the covenant, the acceptance of a sacrifice) that allows the suppliant to pass from his or her distress to gratitude.

Another point of discussion has been the determination of the "I" in these psalms: a) Mowinckel, Eichorn, and Eaton proposed to see the king as the "I" speaking in the name of the whole people, and the enemies would be the enemies of the nation; b) Smend and Kraus proposed a collective interpretation: the "I" is the postexilic community; and c) Balla[6] and Gunkel interpret these psalms as personal expressions of people in distress. This third position is the most classical position and the one that seems most reasonable.

The *Sitz im Leben* of these psalms has also been widely discussed; perhaps the best option is to locate it in the private liturgy spiritually oriented to the temple; they could have been written by professional scribes to whom the suppliant looked in time of distress.

Concerning the Christian appropriation, one can say that the psalms of individual supplication are addressed to God by someone who is in distress and seeks help. As such, these psalms touch a painful but common human reality: suffering. The contribution of these psalms is that through their very simple structure—address to God, description of the suffering, supplication, and thanksgiving (almost always present)—they help to give meaning

Categories of Psalms

to suffering. Far from remaining in a situation of hate against the enemy, or a situation of desperation, the psalm readdresses our heart and mind to the only One who can help us: God.

In addition, these psalms, although originally written for an individual, came to be also a prayer for the whole community, united by their faith and solidarity. Hence, the "I" can be read as a "we" (and vice versa).

To this family belong the following psalms:[7] 5; 6; 7; 13; 17; 22; 25; 26; 27:7–14; 28; 31; 35; 38; 39; 42/43; 51; 54; 55—57; 59; 61; 63; 64; 69; 70 (=40:14–18); 71; 86; 88; 102; 109; 120; 130; 140—143.

EXAMPLE: PSALM 6

STRUCTURE

6:1 *To the leader: with stringed instruments; according to The Sheminith. A Psalm of David.*

6:2 O LORD, do not rebuke me in your anger, or discipline me in your wrath. 6:3 Be gracious to me, O LORD, for I am languishing; O LORD, heal me, for my bones are shaking with terror.	Opening appeal and supplication
6:4 My soul also is struck with terror. while you, O LORD—how long?	Lament or exposition of the case
6:5 Turn, O LORD, save my life; deliver me for the sake of your steadfast love. 6:6 For in death there is no remembrance of you; in Sheol who can give you praise?	Supplication
6:7 I am weary with my moaning; every night I flood my bed with tears; I drench my couch with my weeping. 6:8 My eye wastes away because of grief, they grow weak because of all my foes.	Lament or exposition of the case

6:9 Depart from me, all you workers of evil;
   for the LORD has heard the sound of my
   weeping.
6:10 The LORD has heard my supplication;
   The LORD accepts my prayer.
6:11 All my enemies shall be ashamed and
   struck with terror;
   they shall turn back, and in a moment be
   put to shame.

} Certainty of being heard

LITERARY ANALYSIS

This psalm presents three major elements: a supplication (6:2–3, 5), a lament (6:4, 6–8), and an affirmation of the certainty of being heard (6:9–11). The first person singular is mainly used in the psalm. Therefore, the psalm can be classified among the genre of psalms of individual supplication. Verse 6:3 summarizes the entire psalm:

Be gracious to me, O LORD, for I am languishing;
   O LORD, heal me, for my bones are shaking with terror.

THEOLOGICAL ANALYSIS

The psalmist appears to be afflicted by a physical (v. 3) but also spiritual (v. 4) sickness; this double description is intended to represent the situation of someone who is under the wrath of God: the psalmist is a sinner and therefore has been punished by God. What is to be done in a situation "under the wrath of God" is to go to the physician (cf. Matt 9:12). That is the main theme of the psalm: to move the person to make a supplication to God asking for salvation. But Ps 6 also insists on another idea: the certainty that the supplication will be heard by God.

HISTORICAL ANALYSIS

The language of the psalm suggests that it could have been composed as a prayer for an individual who was very sick, asks for healing, and addresses the prayer either at home or at the temple.

But it was later readapted after the exile for use as prayer of the Jewish community asking for its restoration by God.[8] It has also been suggested that the psalm was composed after the exile, borrowing the style and language of the Book of Jeremiah (which was brought to completion during the exile).[9] But this hypothesis has been criticized[10] on the grounds that the psalm contains formulaic language common to other psalms and books of the OT.[11]

The content of the psalm does not give clues for a certain identification of the *Sitz im Leben* of the psalm. Both—an association of the psalm with the cult at the temple or personal worship—are possible.

Concerning its date of composition, the lack of hope for the afterlife expressed in v. 5 suggests that it is an ancient composition, perhaps preexilic, when the idea of life after death was not yet developed.

NOTES

v. 2 The mention of "anger" and "wrath" implies that the psalmist acknowledges his sin, for the anger of the Lord is the natural consequence (cf. Ps 37:1; Deut 6:14–15; 9:8).

v. 5 The psalmist appeals to the "steadfast love" of the Lord, not to the psalmist's own merits.

v. 6 When there is no remembrance of God, there can be no life; it is the kingdom of death.

v. 11 The enemies will be ashamed because they thought that the one who was appealing to God would be forgotten and die.

CHRISTIAN APPROPRIATION

Since the Christian reader believes in the doctrine of resurrection and everlasting life, the reading of this psalm (especially v. 6) would seem difficult, lest a Christian reading incorporate into the psalm a perspective alien to it. However, based on the theological analysis presented above, we can interpret the psalm as a powerful description of sin and its consequences of being under the wrath of God (6:2), as being in a situation of perennial death (v. 6). But this psalm provides hope at the same time: no matter how bad or desperate our situation, we can ask God for forgiveness and salvation, being fully confident that we will be heard.

This psalm can be prayed by people who are sick, in distress, or anguished by a sinful life, and who hope for a change in their lives. The church has included Ps 6 among its seven penitential psalms (Pss 6; 32; 38; 51; 102; 130; 143).

2. CONFIDENCE PSALMS

These psalms can be considered as a subdivision of the previous category. The motif of confidence in God present in the individual supplications is dominant in these psalms. Generally, the confidence replaces the lamentation or the exposition of the case. They constitute an important expression of personal piety.

Concerning their Christian appropriation, the psalms of confidence, which many consider as a subgenre of the psalms of supplication, remind us that confidence in God should be greater than any difficulty or danger in our lives. Furthermore, they remind us that salvation is ultimately in the hands of the Lord (v. 9).

The following psalms can be considered as belonging to this category: 3; 11; 16; 23; 27:1–6; 41; 62; 131.

EXAMPLE: PSALM 3

STRUCTURE

3:1 *A Psalm of David, when he fled from his son Absalom.*

3:2 O LORD,
   how many are my foes!
   Many are rising against me;
3:3 many are saying to me,
   "There is no help for you in God." [*Selah*]

— Opening appeal that presents the situation

Categories of Psalms

3:4 But you, O LORD, are a shield around me, my glory, and the one who lifts up my head. 3:5 I cry aloud to the LORD, and he answers me from his holy hill. [*Selah*] 3:6 I lie down and sleep; I wake again, for the LORD sustains me. 3:7 I am not afraid of ten thousands of people who have set themselves against me all around.	declaration of confidence
3:8 Arise, O LORD! Deliver me, O my God!	Supplication
For you strike all my enemies on the cheek, you break the teeth of the wicked. 3:9 Deliverance belongs to the LORD; may your blessing be on your people! [*Selah*]	Ratification of confidence

LITERARY GENRE AND HISTORICAL CONTEXT

Psalm 3 is a psalm of supplication in which the dominant theme is confidence in God; hence, it is here classified among the psalms of confidence. When this psalm was incorporated among the Psalms of David (Pss 3—41), it was reinterpreted in the light of the conflict between David and his son Absalom (cf. 2 Sam 15—18). The Psalter presents David as an example of confidence in God: the whole community of Israel should follow his example.

NOTES

3:2-3 The psalm begins by mentioning the confidence of the wicked, who claim that God has forsaken his people; they target the confidence of the psalmist in God. The mention of the "many" (vv. 2-3; cf. "thousands" v. 7) emphasizes the help provided by God mentioned afterward (v. 4).

3:4 Against the attitude of the wicked, the confidence of the righteous stands out, imaginatively described (military images). But perhaps there is an evocation of the promise made to Abraham: "Do not be afraid Abram, I am your shield" (Gen 15:1). According to the prophet Zechariah,

God will protect his people at the time of restoration and deliverance (Zech 12:8).

3:5 "His holy hill" means the temple.

3:6 The Lord watches his people even when they sleep. The mention of the lying down and the awakening (v. 6) describes the amplitude of the confidence (e.g., twenty-four hours).

3:7 The attack of the enemies will fail, because they do not only attempt to go against the psalmist ("against me") but against God, who protects the psalmist (cf. vv. 4, 6); because of this, their move will fail.

3:8 The supplication occupies only half a verse (3:8a); instead, the confidence is the main theme and occupies seven and a half verses. The same mouth that was speaking words against the confidence of the psalmist (3:3) will be hit (3:8b).

3:9 This verse contradicts the statement of the enemies (3:3): salvation is in God and the whole community will benefit from it.

CHRISTIAN APPROPRIATION

Psalm 3 presents in a clear way the main point that could eventually cause the psalmist to stumble: to acknowledge that God has forsaken his people, that God will not assist his people (cf. v. 3). But against such a claim from the enemy, the psalmist proclaims full confidence in God: God is indeed with the believer (cf. v. 4). One can think of the supreme trust of Christ in his Father; in fact, Christian writers have interpreted verse 6 as a reference to Christ's death and resurrection and ask from God the same salvation (v. 8). The symbolic language of the psalm makes it easy to apply it to a number of personal situations, giving assurance to the one who prays, that one can sleep in peace and wake up again (v. 6), no matter how many difficulties and enemies there are.

Categories of Psalms

3. PUBLIC SUPPLICATIONS

These have a similar structure to that of the individual supplications. The difference is that the "I" is replaced by the "we"; the particular case is replaced by a national disaster or calamity. Generally, the community makes present the insults of the enemies, which ultimately are also directed against God. Secondary motifs (not essentials) in these psalms are the prophetic oracle, the evocation of salvific actions of God in the history of Israel, and the use of alternate choirs.

Usually three characters are involved in these psalms: the "we" of the community, the "you" of God, and the "they" of the enemies. The supplication to God is frequently expressed as a question to God: "Why are you asleep?" (Ps 44:24), "Why do you hide your face?" (Ps 44:25), "How long will you be angry, Yahweh?" (Pss 79:5; 80:5 [my translation]); or even as a reproach to God: "You have rejected us" (Ps 44:10). The authors of these psalms do not deny the existence of difficult situations of suffering, but at the same time they seek to put these situations in the hands of God.

Concerning the appropriation, the psalms of public supplication make us think in terms of community: we pray for all, not only for myself alone. The presence of the singular "I" (vv. 7, 8, 16) speaks on behalf of all the people. Indeed, the believer must consider himself or herself as part of the people of God.

The following psalms can be mentioned as belonging to this category: 44; 58; 60.7–14 (=108); 74; 77; 79; 80; 82; 83; 125.

EXAMPLE: PSALM 44

STRUCTURE

44:1 *To the leader. Of the Korahites. A Maskil.*
44:2 We have heard with our ears, O God,
  our ancestors have told us,
  what deeds you performed in their days,
  in the days of old:

The Psalms

44:3 you with your own hand drove out the nations,
  but them you planted;
  you afflicted the peoples,
  but them you set free;
44:4 for not by their own sword did they win the land,
  nor did their own arm give them victory;
  but your right hand, and your arm,
  and the light of your countenance,
  for you delighted in them.
44:5 You are my King and my God;
  you command victories for Jacob.
44:6 Through you we push down our foes;
  through your name we tread down our assailants.
44:7 For not in my bow do I trust,
  nor can my sword save me.
44:8 But you have saved us from our foes,
  and have put to confusion those who hate us.
44:9 In God we have boasted continually,
  and we will give thanks to your name for ever.
  [*Selah*]

Appeal: God's care for Israel

44:10 Yet you have rejected us and abased us,
  and have not gone out with our armies.
44:11 You made us turn back from the foe,
  and our enemies have gotten spoil.
44:12 You have made us like sheep for slaughter,
  and have scattered us among the nations.
44:13 You have sold your people for a trifle,
  demanding no high price for them.
44:14 You have made us the taunt of our neighbours,
  the derision and scorn of those around us.
44:15 You have made us a byword among the nations,
  a laughingstock among the peoples.
44:16 All day long my disgrace is before me,
  and shame has covered my face

Lament: military defeat

Categories of Psalms

44:17 at the words of the taunters and revilers,
at the sight of the enemy and the avenger.

44:18 All this has come upon us,
yet we have not forgotten you,
or been false to your covenant.
44:19 Our heart has not turned back,
nor have our steps departed from your way,
44:20 yet you have broken us in the haunt
of jackals,
and covered us with deep darkness.
44:21 If we had forgotten the name of our God,
or spread out our hands to a strange god,
44:22 would not God discover this?
For he knows the secrets of the heart.
44:23 Because of you we are being killed all
day long,
and accounted as sheep for the slaughter.

Appeal: Israel's innocence

44:24 Rouse yourself! Why do you sleep,
O LORD?
Awake, do not cast us off for ever!
44:25 Why do you hide your face?
Why do you forget our affliction and
oppression?
44:26 For we sink down to the dust;
our bodies cling to the ground.
44:27 Rise up, come to our help.
Redeem us for the sake of your steadfast love.

Supplication

LITERARY GENRE AND HISTORICAL CONTEXT

Psalm 44 is a public supplication after a military disaster.[12] However, it is impossible to identify the situation more precisely.[13] The psalm begins in a positive tone and therefore is misleading; after verse 9 there appears a long recrimination against God. One can distinguish two major parts in the structure of this psalm: contrast between past and present situations (vv. 2–17), and defense and supplication (vv. 18–27). Two things are relevant in this psalm: the affirmation of the people's innocence, and the apparent lack of response from God.

An alternation of speakers is noticeable in the structure of the psalm, suggesting that the psalm was composed to be sung in alternate voices (soloist and choir):[14]

1st part: appeal	2nd & 3rd part: lament & appeal	4th part: supplication
the people vv. 2–4	the people vv. 10–15	king & people vv. 24–27
the king v. 5	the king vv. 16–17	
the people v. 6	the people vv. 18–23	
the king v. 7		
the people vv. 8–9		

NOTES

vv. 2–9 This is recollection of past events when God saved his people. This is the reason why the psalmist asks God to continue such a history of salvation. As God had given victories to Jacob (v. 5) (i.e., Israel), this is expected as well for the present. The affirmation of verse 7 presents orthodox theology: only God saves, and therefore only God deserves to be praised and thanked (v. 9).

vv. 10–17 We shift now from the happy past to the present adverse situation; the repeated use of the pronoun "you" indicates the use of judicial language, giving the responsibility to God (cf. the repetition of the words, "You have…" vv. 10–15). Notable here is the Semitic idea of attributing everything to the first cause: God. In fact, God has been responsible for the salvation of the people (vv. 2–9), and God is also responsible for the defeat of the people (vv. 10–17). The disgrace has fallen upon the people (vv. 10–15) and upon the king as its representative (vv. 16–17).

vv. 18–23 The affirmation of their own innocence stands out in this psalm; the psalmist does not understand the reason for the disgrace described before (vv. 10–17). The purpose of the covenant was the fidelity to God (v. 18) but such fidelity is now the cause of persecution (v. 23). The people have neither forgotten the covenant (v. 18) nor broken the first commandment (v. 21) or lied to God (v. 22). The theological understanding of the covenant is shaken: they had expected to be saved by God, but what has happened is the opposite (v. 20).

vv. 24-27 In contrast with Job, who fought against God, there is only a cry of supplication full of confidence in God. In front of such an incomprehensible situation, the only thing the people do is to appeal to God. The people entreat God that God will not reject them "forever" (v. 24). The supplication is mixed with a lament, "Why…?" (v. 25) to give force to the supplication. The mention of God's love (v. 27) is the ultimate reason for appealing for God's intervention. Against the incomprehensible situation, the cry of the psalmist in Ps 44 shows that faith is rooted in something else beyond logical reason. This psalm opens up the mystery of God.

The final redactors or editors of the collection of "the psalms of the sons of Korah" have put Pss 45—48 as God's answer to the cry of Ps 44:23-26. As a matter of fact, a number of words are repeated in all these psalms: a) the work of the Lord (44:3; 46:9), b) "your right hand" (44:4; 48:10), c) "my King" (44:5; 47:2, 6, 7), d) "Jacob" (44:5; 46:7; 47:4), e) "your name" (44:9; 48:10), f) "bow" (44:7; 46:9), g) God's help (44:27; 46:1,5), and h) "your steadfast love" (44:27; 48:9).

CHRISTIAN APPROPRIATION

This psalm seems to give the opposite idea to that of the psalms of confidence: it ends with an urgent cry for help (v. 27). The answer, however, is not given in this psalm but in the next one: in Ps 45 the Lord appears as a victorious king coming to his people, and is united to it as a bride to his bridegroom, and she will give birth to many children. Therefore, Ps 44 reminds us that every book of the Bible has to be read and interpreted in the context of the whole Bible. In the same way that Ps 44 prepares for Ps 45, so the OT prepares the way for the NT.

This psalm also serves as a warning to any believer: is it that we praise God only when things go well (vv. 2-9) but complain against God when things go the opposite way (vv. 10-17)? The right attitude would be not to appeal to our innocence (vv.

18–23) but to put our trust in God (vv. 24–27). This psalm does not give an answer to the mystery of the suffering of the righteous, but it does give good advice: trust God. St. Paul applies verse 23 to all Christians (cf. Rom 8:36).

4. THANKSGIVING PSALMS

These psalms manifest the joyful acknowledgment of one who has been heard by God; they constitute the complement to the supplication psalms. The essential elements of this kind of psalm are:

1. *Opening*: An introductory formula that expresses the will and opportunity for thanking God. This formula sets the tone for the whole psalm.
2. *Body*: The psalmist mentions a) the danger, sickness, or misfortune from which he or she has been saved; b) the cry for help addressed to God; and c) the help received. So, the psalmist gives reason for his or her thanksgiving. Characteristic is the use of the Hebrew word (אורה *'ôdeh*), which can be translated as, "I thank," "I confess" (namely, "the goodness of God"), or "I offer."
3. *Conclusion*: A praise that concludes the psalm. However, not all the psalms of this kind have a conclusion that can be separated from the body of the psalm.

It has been suggested that the *Sitz im Leben* of these psalms be considered to be the time when the suppliant is in the temple offering the sacrifice for having being heard, and saying or singing one of these psalms; moreover, the thanksgiving psalm could perhaps be said by the suppliant or by the Levites in his name. However, these psalms did not necessarily have the temple as origin, since some thanksgiving psalms could be composed far away from the temple, but always as an expression of piety and gratitude.

This category of psalms is similar to that of the hymns; the difference is that here the author does not rigorously follow a schema, but uses a freer structure. In the NT these psalms are represented by the Magnificat (Luke 1:46-55) and the Benedictus (Luke 1:68-79).

Concerning the appropriation, the considerable number of psalms of thanksgiving (at least thirteen psalms) remind us how important it is to thank God for the benefits we receive (cf. Luke 17:16-18); they also help us to express our recognition to God with beautiful words. The images used (Sheol, pit, dismay, death, mourning, restoration, weeping, joy, face, sackcloth) allow us to apply the psalms to a variety of situations. The psalms of thanksgiving appear as a completion to the idea presented by the psalms of supplication: God indeed listens to the cry for help.

The thanksgiving psalms can be divided as follows:

- Private thanksgivings: 4; 18; 30; 32; 34; 40:2-11; 66; 92; 116; 118; 138
- Public thanksgivings: 124; 129.

EXAMPLE: PSALM 30

STRUCTURE

30:1 *A Psalm. A Song at the dedication of the temple. Of David.*

30:2 I will extol you, O LORD, for you have drawn me up, and did not let my foes rejoice over me.	Opening: praise + reason (to thank s. for s.)
30:3 O LORD my God, I cried to you for help, and you have healed me. 30:4 O LORD, you brought up my soul from Sheol, restored me to life from among those gone down to the Pit.	Reason for giving thanks
30:5 Sing praises to the LORD, O you his faithful ones, and give thanks to his holy name. 30:6 For his anger is but for a moment; his favor is for a lifetime.	Invitation to give thanks

> Weeping may linger for the night,
> but joy comes with the morning.

> 30:7 As for me, I said in my prosperity,
> "I shall never be moved."
> 30:8 By your favor, O Lord,
> you had established me as a strong mountain;
> you hid your face;
> I was dismayed.
> 30:9 To you, O Lord, I cried,
> and to the Lord I made supplication:
> 30:10 "What profit is there in my death,
> if I go down to the Pit?
> Will the dust praise you?
> Will it tell of your faithfulness?
> 30:11 Hear, O Lord, and be gracious to me!
> O Lord, be my helper!"

— Recollection of the previous situation of danger and cry for help

> 30:12 You have turned my mourning into dancing;
> you have taken off my sackcloth
> and clothed me with joy,
> 30:13 so that my soul may praise you and not be silent.

— Memory of the help received

> O Lord, my God, I will give thanks to you for ever.

— Thanksgiving promise

LITERARY GENRE AND HISTORICAL SETTING

Psalm 30 was originally a personal prayer that was reused at a later time as a communal prayer on the occasion of the dedication of the temple in 164 BC by the Maccabees (1 Macc 4:50–56).[15] The theme of the psalm allowed for this readaptation: from describing restoration from sickness and the sin of self-confidence; the psalm was later read in the context of the reestablishment of the covenant, as the community of Israel was passing from death to life. In fact, the covenant promise of God was life, and death was its antithesis (cf. Deut 30:15–20). Concerning the description of the sickness, the psalm has parallels with Hezekiah's prayer (Isa 38:10–28).

Westermann has proposed that this psalm should be considered as a psalm of praise, given the initial words "I will extol you" (v. 2; see also v. 5a, 13a), but since the psalmist refers to a saving act of God in the past (vv. 3–4, 12), it is better to consider it as a thanksgiving psalm (so also: Fohrer, Schreiner).

NOTES[16]

- v. 2 This verse summarizes the whole psalm: the psalmist will extol Yahweh as a consequence of deliverance from death and enemies. Note the relationship between "I will extol you" and "You have drawn me up." It is possible to think that the enemies have provoked the situation of death and, therefore, they laugh; but it is better to understand the words "my foes rejoice" simply in the sense that they laugh because the psalmist is sick.
- vv. 3–4 The reference to a past situation of anguish (v. 3a) and the salvific intervention of God (vv. 3b–4) indicate clearly that the psalm should be classified as an individual thanksgiving psalm. The expression "from Sheol" describes a situation of sickness that was already leading to death.
- v. 5 The "faithful ones" are the *hasidim*: fellow members of the covenant community who have experienced mercy (*hesed*) from God.
- v. 6 The psalmist believes that the time of trial or suffering is only a means for purification, not to destroy the faithful. The anger is the divine response to sin, but God's favor is the divine response to goodness and to repentance. The mention of the "night" is to be taken symbolically: the dark night is the time of experiencing the anger of God, which in the end leads to repentance. The morning is the symbol of salvation.
- v. 7 In the context of the covenant, self-confidence was the fundamental sin: to think that success was a human achievement and not a gift from God (cf. Deut 8:17–18).

The Psalms

vv. 7–13 The recollection of the time of proof or suffering is an essential part of the thanksgiving psalms. The psalmist thought that nothing would happen to him or her (vv. 7–8a); it was perhaps a too materialistic understanding of the favor of God (cf. Job 1:1–3). Being at the point of death (v. 10) made the situation of anguish even more acute (v. 8b).

v. 8 The psalmist presents the real state of affairs that contrasts the foolishness of the previous thought (v. 7). The contrast is reinforced through an antithetical parallelism (vv. 7–8a). This rethinking of the situation explains what the psalmist affirmed in verse 6: God's action was only a correction against self-confidence.

v. 9 But the psalmist reacts and seeks help from God (vv. 9, 11); that is the turning point in the psalm.

vv. 9–11 These verses could refer to a previous prayer addressed at the temple. The language of the psalm is reminiscent of other prayers (compare v. 9 with Pss 28:1; 142:1; compare v. 10 with Pss 6:5; 88:10–12; 115:17).

v. 10 The psalmist presents the reasons for the supplication. It is implied that the psalmist has repented. So, the logic is this: How will the psalmist be able then to praise God from Sheol? The logic adduced reveals that the belief in the afterlife was not yet accepted; this would suggest a preexilic or early postexilic origin of the psalm. The psalmist does not ask for healing but for the opportunity to praise God; the spiritual healing is given priority over the physical healing. To return to a state of physical welfare but without repentance (v. 7), would be useless.

v. 11 This verse presents the actual request to God.

vv. 12–13 The response from the Lord is speedy.

v. 13 The situation of the psalmist did not just improve as before, but above all she or he has had a renewal of spiritual health. The psalm ends as it began: praising God. The final verse (v. 13b) announces the conclusion, to thank the Lord forever. The action of thanking God is not limited to an instant, but is to be continued "forever."

Categories of Psalms

CHRISTIAN APPROPRIATION

Psalm 30 provides important ideas: a) we should not interpret the favor of God in too materialistic terms (vv. 7–8a); b) in time of distress, we should always put our trust in God (vv. 9, 11); c) we should consider the times of suffering and trial as time of purification (cf. v. 6); and d) we should never doubt that the Lord will certainly listen to our cry for help (vv. 3–4).

5. HYMNS

The hymn is disinterested praise, oriented not to ask for something but to praise. This category is well represented in the Book of Psalms. In fact the entire Psalter is called in the Hebrew Bible "Songs of Praise" (תהילים, *tehîllîm*).

The formal elements of the hymns are:

1. *Introduction*: Ordinarily an invitation to praise, an indication to adopt particular attitudes or to use instruments in a precise way. This can be done in several ways: a) through the use of imperatives like, "Sing!," "Praise!," "Shout!," "Celebrate!," "Acclaim!," applied to God, his name, his attributes, his works, and so on; or imperatives like, "Give glory!," "Adore!," and so forth; or exhortatives (cohortatives)[17] like, "Bless [Yahweh, my soul]!" when the psalmist invites the community together with himself or herself to praise God. b) The solemn mention of the act of praise: "The heavens are telling the glory of God" (Ps 19:1). c) The proclamation of the goodness or majesty of God: "Yahweh, how majestic is your name" (Ps 8:1, translation altered).
2. *Body*: It is usually introduced by the Hebrew word (כי *kî* "because," "since," "for"), which gives the reason or cause for the praise. God is praised because of his name, his glory, his goodness, his works, and so on; the real motif of praise is in God himself. Sometimes the participle is also used: "He who forgives," "He who redeems" (Ps 103:3–4, translation altered).

3. *Conclusion*: It can have different forms: echoing the whole content of the psalm, echoing the initial formulae of the hymn, or presenting the hymn to God and asking for its acceptance.

The *Sitz im Leben* of the hymns is generally the cult: there are allusions to the temple (Ps 100:4), to the song or music (Ps 33:2-3), to the pilgrimage (Ps 122:1-4), to the liturgical ritual (Ps 81:3-4). In this liturgical feast, the people participates with the cry הללויה *halelûyāh* ("Praise God"; Pss 106:1; 11:1; 112:1; 113:1; 146:1; 147:1; 148:1; 149:1; 150:1, 6). However, the *Sitz im Leben* can also be independent of the temple. Sometimes the atmosphere is solemn and magnificent, and sometimes it is intimate, full of admiration of and meditation on God and his works.

Concerning our appropriation of these psalms, we can say that the hymns are praises of God detached of any other personal interest; they do not seek a favor from God, but only to praise God. They offer various reasons: God's care for the people, God's power, God's mercy, and so on. They remind us that at the center of our faith it is only God for what God is. It is notable that the last psalm of the Psalter is a hymn that ends with an invitation to praise God: "Let everything that breathes praise the LORD!" (Ps 150:6).

The following psalms can be classified under the "hymns" category: 8; 19; 29; 33; 65; 67; 68; 85; 100; 103; 104; 111; 113; 114; 117; 135; 136; 145—150. However, the "Zion Psalms" and "Yahweh is King Psalms" (see below) can also be considered under the category of hymns.

EXAMPLE: PSALM 8 (TRANSLATION MODIFIED)

STRUCTURE

8:1 *To the leader: according to The Gittith. A Psalm of David.*

8:2 O LORD, our Sovereign, how majestic is your name in all the earth!	Introduction: praise to God

Categories of Psalms

> You have set your glory above the heavens. ⎫
> 8:3 Out of the mouths of babes and infants ⎪
>   you have founded a bulwark because of ⎬ Reason: the
>   your foes, ⎪ creation of
>   to silence the enemy and the avenger. ⎪ the world
> 8:4 When I look at your heavens, the work of ⎪
>   your fingers, ⎪
>   the moon and the stars that you have ⎪
>   established; ⎭
>
> 8:5 what is man that you are mindful of him, ⎫
>   and the son of man that you care for him? ⎬ weakness
> 8:6 Yet you have made them a little lower ⎪
>   than God, ⎭
>   and crowned them with glory and honor. ⎫ Reason:
> 8:7 You have given them dominion over the ⎪ creation of
>   works of your hands; ⎬ greatness humankind
> you have put all things under their feet, ⎪
> 8:8 all sheep and oxen, ⎪
>   and also the beasts of the field, ⎪
> 8:9 the birds of the air, and the fish of the sea, ⎪
>   whatever passes along the paths of the seas. ⎭
>
> 8:10 O LORD, our Sovereign, ⎫ Conclusion: repetition
>   how majestic is your name in all the earth! ⎭ of initial praise

LITERARY GENRE AND HISTORICAL CONTEXT

This is the first hymn in the Psalter. It is difficult to say whether this psalm was composed for the cult at the temple[18] or for another setting, such as to comfort the Jewish communities in exile.[19] The created universe occupies a major role in this psalm, and, therefore, some have seen an influence from the wisdom tradition in it. However, the mention of creation is secondary to the mention of the "name" of God. In this psalm, creation is not the means through which God is revealed, but sets the condition for God's revelation: it evokes the sense of nothingness that must precede God's revelation.[20] This psalm also offers a theological anthropology: when humankind recognizes God, then it finds its full dignity.

NOTES

v. 2 The universe is designated by the mention of the "earth" and "heavens." The "name" of Yahweh evokes God's revelation to Israel (cf. Exod 3:15) and the care for his people.[21] However, the text of the hymn does not mention Israel, and hence it can be easily applied to all humanity.

v. 3 The weak speech of "babes" has a strength greater than the arrogant speech of the "foes," when they take the "name" of God in their lips. Hence, God uses the weak of this world to show his strength and put "to silence" his enemies. This image sets the stage for what follows: God has given to the smallness of humanity (v. 5) the power and strength over creation (vv. 6–9).

vv. 4–5 The transition between the two main parts of the body of the psalm is relevant: the dignity of the human being (vv. 5–9) is based on the lordship of God over the whole creation (vv. 2b–4). The dignity of the human being is presented as part of the order of the creation. Human strength is only God's gift, not something earned by mere human success.

v. 5 After describing the vastness of the universe and the stars (v. 4), the logical conclusion is the rhetorical question of wonder: "What is man?" (אנוש, *'ĕnôsh;* ἄνθρωπος *anthrōpos* v. 5). The expression "son of man" is synonymous with "mortal." The implied answer is, "Nothing!"

vv. 6–9 The question of verse 5 seeks to put emphasis on the positive answer of verses 6–9. Some ancient versions (LXX, Syr, Tg, Vg) have translated the Hebrew word *Elohim* in v. 6 by "angels," although the Greek versions of Symmachus and Aquila translated "God."

v.10 The revelation of God's name has given a new awareness to human existence in the framework of creation. Verses 10 and 2 form an inclusion that frames the whole psalm.

Categories of Psalms

CHRISTIAN APPROPRIATION

Psalm 8 reminds us that human nature is not valued in itself (as in Greek culture), but as a gift from God. It is because of God's will that humankind rules over the earth. Human dignity is founded on the majesty and graciousness of God, and nothing should challenge such dignity. Human dignity may not be subjected to racial discrimination, social status, age, sex, and the like. This idea was important at the time of the first generation of Christians (cf. Gal 3:28) and should also be important in our time. St. Paul will add one more reason to uphold the dignity of the human being: the love of Christ (cf. Rom 14:15). Psalm 8 formulates a theological anthropology that leads to the recognition of God (v. 10); the antithesis of this attitude is the standpoint of the sinner (cf. Ps 14). The human being is truly a person when he or she acknowledges God as Creator and Lord.

About the relationship between Ps 8 (hymn) and the previous Pss 6–7 (individual supplications), one can ask, how is it possible to reconcile the greatness of the human person (Ps 8) and his or her sufferings (Pss 6–7)? Suffering and glory are not incompatible (cf. Matt 16:21; John 12:24; Phil 2:5–11).

In the NT, Jesus quotes Ps 8:3 in reference to the children who acclaim his triumphal entrance to Jerusalem (Palm Sunday) (Matt 21:16): the children take the "name" upon their lips, but the Jewish authorities (who play the role of the enemies in Ps 8:3) are indignant. But in both cases (Ps 8:3 and Matt 21:16), it is the little ones who have the true perception.[22]

6. ZION PSALMS

The structure of these psalms is the same as of the hymns. The praise of Zion, the holy city of God, is the characteristic element (Pss 46:5; 48:2–4, 12–14; 50:2; 87:2–3, 5; 97:8; 99:2). The fact that Zion is the chosen city of God establishes a thematic link between these psalms and hymns, where the direct praise of God is characteristic. These psalms are related to the psalms of the fidelity of Yahweh since Zion is the symbol of the election of the people by

God; they are also related to the royal psalms since the king resides in Zion.

The following psalms can be classified under this category: Pss 24; 46; 48; 76; 84; 87; 122; 137. They can be divided into two groups: a) some psalms praise Zion as the transfigured capital of the messianic kingdom in its moment of fight or victory against its enemies (Pss 46; 48; 76); b) others, however, praise Zion as the preferred city of God in its moment of definite triumph (Pss 84; 87; 122).

The *Sitz im Leben* of the first group is to be seen in a concrete historical situation. So, for example, the defeat of Sennacherib in 701 BC is probably to be seen as the background for Ps 46; Ps 48 also could refer to the same event, not immediately following the victory but at a some later time when the troops of Sennacherib were gone. Psalm 76 probably refers to the same victory over Sennacherib. The *Sitz im Leben* of the second group can be seen as the main national cultic feasts, where the majesty and glory of Zion as the chosen city of God is celebrated.

Gunkel classified Pss 84 and 122 under the special category of "Psalms of Ascents," psalms to be sung by the pilgrims going up to Jerusalem. Other scholars include Pss 120—134 under this category, since the title of these psalms is Psalms of Ascent (שיר המעלוח, *shîr hamma'ălôt*). These psalms would be sung during the feasts of pilgrimage (Passover, Weeks or Pentecost, and Shelters or Tabernacles; cf. Exod 23:14–19) to the temple in Jerusalem.[23]

The precise understanding of these psalms of ascent is, however, debated. Some scholars understand them in the context of the return to Jerusalem after the exile. Castellino considers them as psalms to be sung during the first day of the Feast of the Tabernacles or Tents. Others understand the ascent as the ascent of the pilgrim toward the temple in Jerusalem. Is this a homogeneous group? Even on this there is no agreement. E. Beaucamp affirms its unity, but K. Seybold holds that they were different psalms gathered under the title of "psalms of ascent."

Concerning their appropriation, the Psalms of Zion praise and sing the presence of God among his people. They also encourage us to seek our final home, the heavenly Zion, and remind us the beauty of it.

Categories of Psalms

EXAMPLE: PSALM 122

STRUCTURE

122:1 *A Song of Ascents. Of David.*

I was glad when they said to me, "Let us go to the house of the LORD!" 122:2 Our feet are standing within your gates, O Jerusalem.		Introduction: joy of departure and arrival
122:3 Jerusalem—built as a city that is bound firmly together. 122:4 To it the tribes go up, the tribes of the LORD,	admiration of the city	Praise of Zion
as was decreed for Israel, to give thanks to the name of the LORD. 122:5 For there the thrones for judgement were set up the thrones of the house of David.	reason: its holiness & social relevance	
122:6 Pray for the peace of Jerusalem: "May they prosper who love you. 122:7 Peace be within your walls, and security within your towers."	good wishes to the city	Invitation to pray for Zion
122:8 For the sake of my relatives and friends I will say, "Peace be within you." 122:9 For the sake of the house of the LORD our God, I will seek your good.	good wishes to all	

LITERARY GENRE AND HISTORICAL CONTEXT

This psalm of Zion is remarkable for its deep personal tone (cf. v. 1). The first and last verses of the psalm make clear that the praise of Jerusalem is God-centered.[24] This psalm forms part of the "Psalms of Ascents" (Pss 120—134). The psalmist appears as a pilgrim to the holy city (vv. 1–2). The mention of a pilgrimage to

Zion, where the administration of justice will be made (v. 5), is present also in Isaiah 2:2–4 (= Mic 4:1–3).

The dating of the psalm is subject to debate.[25] Its high praise for Jerusalem suggests that it was composed before the exile.[26] And the allusion to a centralized cult (v. 4) favors a post-Deuteronomic date (i.e., after 622 BC) (cf. Deut 12:5; 2 Kgs 23).[27] However, the interest in going up to Jerusalem in pilgrimage dates to an earlier time: right after the division of the two kingdoms (1 Kgs 12:27–28).[28] But we cannot discount the possibility of seeing some degree of idealization of Jerusalem in the psalm and dating it at a postexilic period.[29]

NOTES

Ps 122 A composition in distichs (pairs of lines of verse), is a hymn to Zion made by a pilgrim to the holy city. In fact, the Law required every Jew to go up to Jerusalem (cf. Deut 16:16).

vv. 1–2 These two verses mention the departure and arrival to Jerusalem, the city of Zion; they are the two extremes of the life of the Israelite: to listen to the invitation to go to the city of God (passive stage), and to walk to the city (active). The joy is mentioned in each case, making omission of all the fatigue and pain of the journey.

vv. 3–5 The main section of the psalm praises the glory of Zion: well established by God (v. 3), center of cult of all the tribes (v. 4), and where justice is made (v. 5), since true cult and worship of God cannot be dissociated from justice (as the prophets emphasized; cf. Amos 5:21–24). The "thrones" are those of the judges and kings.

v. 4 The "decree for Israel" is perhaps the one in Deuteronomy 16:16: the Jew had to go up to Jerusalem as stated in the law. In this case, the psalm could not be earlier than the seventh century BC.[30]

vv. 6–9 The peace (mentioned three times) is the sum of all blessings (cf. Ps 29:11). It is wished for Jerusalem ("city of peace," cf. Ps 76:3)[31] since she is the "house of…God" (v. 9). It was the Jewish custom to offer greetings of peace on entering a home (cf. 1 Sam 25:6; Matt 10:12–13).

CHRISTIAN APPROPRIATION

Psalm 122 reminds us that the blessing of peace (three times) has its roots in the house of God. And that peace comprises the relationship with God (the worship at the temple of Jerusalem) and the relationship among people (the seat for the thrones of judgment).

In the Middle Ages, theologians looked for the four senses of Scripture: Jerusalem is a city to which they travel (literal sense); any place where pilgrims gather together for internal cleansing and prayer to God, as, for example, the church (allegorical sense); our soul where we pray to God (moral sense); and heaven (mystical sense).[32]

7. "YAHWEH IS KING" PSALMS

These psalms (together with the Zion Psalms) can also be considered as a subdivision of the hymns. In fact, they have the same structure as that of the hymns. The reason we assign them to a different category is their characteristic insistence on portraying Yahweh as King: "God reigns" (מלך אלהים, *mālak 'ĕlōhîm*, Ps 47:9, translation modified); "Yahweh reigns" (יהוה מלך, *Yahweh mālāk*, Ps 93:1, translation modified).[33] Also, in these psalms the universal dominion or rule of God over all the peoples is proclaimed (Pss 47:3b, 8; 93:1-2; 96:10; 97:1; 99:1-2). The description of God as judge over his people is also present in some of these psalms (e.g., Pss 75:7; 96:10; 97:2), because judgment was one of the duties of the king (cf. 1 Kgs 3:28). Besides, God is to reign over a holy people, not over a sinful people, and therefore has to purify his people, rejecting the wicked and the sinner (cf. Pss 75:10; 97:10-12; 99:8).

The *Sitz im Leben* of these psalms is perhaps to be seen in the joyful proclamation of Yahweh as King after a victory over the enemies of his people, and in that way affirming his dominion over all the peoples. The psalms of the kingship of Yahweh seem to have originated in the preexilic period as the Israelites celebrated the victories of Yahweh upon all other nations, in particular the Egyptians (Exod 15:18; Num 23:21-22) and the Canaanites (Ps 47:4). For the Israelites, Yahweh is King as he provides salvation (Isa 52:7; Ezek 20:33-37; Ps 98:2) and redemption (Isa 44:6) to his people.

These psalms later became part of the annual liturgy,[34] detaching themselves from the original historical situation in which they were born, looking forward to the "day of Yahweh," when God will make a definitive intervention in history. These psalms therefore acquired a messianic and eschatological dimension (cf. Dan 2:44). In the other books of the OT, the idea of the kingship of Yahweh is presented only in exilic and postexilic texts; this idea is clearly presented, for example, in Second Isaiah (Isa 41:21; 43:15; 52:7).

Concerning their appropriation, the psalms of the kingship of Yahweh exalt the power of God over all creation. They invite us to recognize God as the Lord over all creation. That should be a motif to live with joy. We know that we are in the hands of a righteous King (Ps 99:3) who saves his people (Ps 47:4).

The following psalms can be considered under this category: Pss 47; 75; 93; 96—99.

EXAMPLE: PSALM 47

STRUCTURE

47:1 *To the leader. Of the Korahites. A Psalm.*

47:2 Clap your hands, all you peoples;
   shout to God with loud songs of joy.

— Introduction: invitation to praise God

47:3 For the LORD, the Most High, is awesome,
   a great king over all the earth.
47:4 He subdued peoples under us,
   and nations under our feet.
47:5 He chose our heritage for us,
   the pride of Jacob whom he loves. [*Selah*]
47:6 God has gone up with a shout,
   the LORD with the sound of a trumpet.

— Reason: Yahweh is king

Categories of Psalms

47:7 Sing praises to God, sing praises; sing praises to our King, sing praises. 47:8 For God is the king of all the earth; sing praises with a psalm.	Renewed invitation to praise God
47:9 God is king over the nations; God sits on his holy throne. 47:10 The princes of the peoples gather as the people of the God of Abraham. For the shields of the earth belong to God; he is highly exalted.	Reason: Yahweh is King

LITERARY GENRE

This psalm was classified by Mowinckel as a Psalm of enthronement of Yahweh (v. 9), proper to the celebration of the new year. But the problem with this designation is that there are no clear references in the Bible to an enthronement of Yahweh during the celebration of this feast.[35] Besides, there are some psalms that have the kingship of Yahweh as their theme and do not present the idea of a procession to the throne (e.g., Pss 75; 98). Therefore, it is perhaps preferable to use, as do Castellino and Sabourin, a broader title for this kind of psalm: "Hymn of the Kingship of Yahweh." Furthermore, the term *enthronement* seems to give the idea of Yahweh "becoming" King, while in reality, God is King.

HISTORICAL CONTEXT

There have been many suggestions as to the original context of this hymn of the kingship of Yahweh: a) as an accompaniment to the procession of the ark into the temple (v. 6) at the feast of the new year; b) or, on the other hand, at the feast of the renewal of the covenant; c) the celebration of the conquest of Canaan (vv. 4-5) during the time of the monarchy; d) the dedication of the Solomonic temple (v. 6, cf. 1 Kgs 8); e) the time of the conquests of David (v. 2, cf. 2 Sam 8:9-12) or Solomon (v. 2, cf. 1 Kgs 5:1); f) after the exile, since there is no mention of a Davidic king, and because of its universalism; or g) on the other hand, this universalism may be a sign of its antiquity. The variety of these suggestions indicates the difficulty in determining the precise historical context.

The idea of relating the hymn to the conquest of Canaan (vv. 4–5) seems to be the best option. This intervention of God in the early history of Israel would have been repeated and actualized in other events of the history of Israel (e.g., the victories of David and Solomon), and therefore the hymn could be repeated and enriched through time. This way, the hymn relates to the major events of the history of Israel, through which God revealed his power and glory, as the only King.

One can distinguish two parts in this psalm, each of which is divided into two other sections. While the first part (vv. 2–6) probably recalls the conquest of Canaan and could be sung at the procession to the temple (cf. "God has gone up" v. 6), the second part (vv. 7–10) seems to recall the consequences of the conquest (God is King over all nations) and could be sung in the liturgy at the temple (cf. "God sits on his holy throne" v. 9).

NOTES

- v. 2 The invitation is to all peoples; the universalism is emphasized in this psalm (cf. vv. 8–9). Because of this idea, the psalm was considered as an eschatological praise, looking to the future.
- v. 3 Since Yahweh[36] is the Most High, Yahweh appears as King not only upon Israel but upon all nations.
- v. 4 Notice the reference to concrete facts and not myths (in contrast to the Canaanite religion).
- v. 5 The universal power of God and his election of Israel appear to be associated.
- v. 6 Some interpret the "ascension" of God as a ritual procession with the holy ark in which God is taken into the temple, to finally sit on his throne (cf. v. 9). The use of the trumpet was at the time of the proclamation of the new king (cf. 2 Sam 15:10; 1 Kgs 1:38–40; 2 Kgs 9:13)
- v. 10 The covenant with Abraham is extended to embrace all nations (cf. Gen 12:2–3; 15:5; 17:2–6).

Categories of Psalms

CHRISTIAN APPROPRIATION

This psalm makes us reflect on the relationship between election and universal grace: While some could say that God is the God of Israel, why does the psalmist invite all nations to acknowledge God as their king (47:2–3)?

Psalm 8 begins praising the universal dominion of Yahweh over all the world (v. 2), but as it underlines the election of Israel (v. 4), it seems to narrow its view. However, the psalm ends by declaring that the people of Abraham is not defined by its ethnicity but by the recognition of Yahweh's kingship (v. 9). Hence, Ps 8 considers the election of Israel only as a means of inviting all nations to recognize Yahweh as king. When God chooses someone, it is in order to render a service to all, not a privilege. St. Paul appealed to that idea for describing the mystery of the election of Israel in Romans 9—11.

The eschatological dimension of the psalm, which looks to the universal reign of God, was considered by Christians as already being partially fulfilled with Christ (cf. Acts 2:8–12).

8. ROYAL (AND MESSIANIC) PSALMS

These psalms are thematically connected with the previous psalms, since the king resides in Zion (Zion Psalms) and is frequently seen as the earthly representative of God, the supernatural king (Kingship of Yahweh Psalms).

This group includes prayers in favor of the king (Pss 20; 21; 72; 89), prayers of the king himself (Pss 18; 101; 144), and prayers celebrating special moments of the king (Ps 45) or his victories (Pss 2; 110). Therefore, the *Sitz im Leben* of these psalms is probably a cultic celebration in connection with the king, as for example the feast for the coronation (anointing) of the new king or the anniversary of the coronation.

The monarchic institution in ancient Israel was not a mere political fact, but an event with deep religious dimension. The king was consecrated by the anointing, in which the Spirit of Yahweh was given to him; this way the king was adopted as son and became the agent of God on earth.[37] The day of the coronation was then considered as the day of the birth of the adoptive son of Yahweh, receiving the mission of governing with justice (ṣĕdāqāh) and judgment (mishpāṭ).[38]

Because the Davidic king was the qualified representative of God and adopted by him (Ps 2:7), the royal psalms easily go beyond the human sphere and describe the supernatural reality of the Messiah and his eschatological kingdom. Some psalms praise the Messiah's extraordinary kingship and dominion (Pss 2; 22; 72; 90; 110). This description can be complemented with other psalms that praise the kingdom of God and its place in history (Pss 47; 76; 85; 87; 96; 98; 99; etc.). This situation paved the road for the fact that the literal sense of some royal psalms (the messianic psalms)[39] could be taken in the typological sense in the light of the event of Christ.

Historically speaking, the preaching of Jesus on the kingdom of God (Mark 1:14–15) was perhaps one of the motifs that prompted the people to recognize him as Messiah, that is, king. In that context, the address of Jesus to God as his Father may have been understood as an evocation of 2 Samuel 7:14.[40] But the main event that moved NT authors to recognize Christ as the Messiah, the king, the Son of God (cf. Rom 1:4), was Jesus' resurrection.

These psalms do not follow a fixed pattern; however, we can mention some frequent themes and stylistic elements:

1. *Oracle*: The divine decree addressed to the king (*Königsprotokoll*) (cf. Pss 2:7–9; 110:1, 3–4).
2. *Dynastic Promise*: The divine promise given to David and his dynasty (cf. Pss 20:2–6; 72:1–2; 132:1–2, 10).
3. *Supplication for the king*: An appeal to God to help and protect the king.

Some scholars consider these psalms as a literary fiction of the postexilic period, detached of any earthly king because the monarchy no longer existed; they would have had only the scope of expressing hope in the Messiah, or the future ideal king.

Categories of Psalms

According to these authors (e.g., A. Robert, R. Tournay, and A. Deissler), these psalms are messianic in their literal sense. More plausible, however, is Gunkel's dating of these psalms to the time of the preexilic monarchy and the suggestion that the royal psalms had reelaborations in the postexilic period. Moreover, it is likely, as Castellino suggests,[41] that some royal psalms were interpreted in a messianic sense already in the monarchical period: the people would expect that the promise made to David would be a reality with the enthronement of the new king. Reality would later show that the promise still had to wait for its fulfillment. So, during the exilic and postexilic period the messianic oracle was spiritualized and eschatologized.

Concerning their appropriation, the royal psalms have the king as their main theme, and therefore could seem a thing of the past, without relevance for our time. But if we consider that the king was the representative of the people,[42] we can pray these psalms, applying them to all the people of God, the community of believers.[43] But above all, the royal psalms can be read in the light of Christ as the Messiah; this is even more prominent in the group of messianic psalms. Hence, these psalms appear as messianic meditations that help us to understand the mystery of Christ's redemption.

The following psalms can be classified under the category of royal psalms: 2; 20; 21; 45; 72; 89; 101; 110; 132; 144. Psalm 18 is also a royal psalm but perhaps it is better to classify it as a Thanksgiving Psalm.

EXAMPLE: PSALM 2

STRUCTURE

2:1 Why do the nations conspire,
    and the peoples plot in vain?
2:2 The kings of the earth set themselves,
    and the rulers take counsel together,
    against the Lord and his anointed, saying,
2:3 "Let us burst their bonds asunder,
    and cast their cords from us."
	Introduction: revolt of the vassal kings on occasion of the change of ruler

The Psalms

2:4 He who sits in the heavens laughs;
    the LORD has them in derision.
2:5 Then he will speak to them in his wrath,
    and terrify them in his fury, saying,
2:6 "I have set my king on Zion, my holy hill."
	Response from God: oracle on behalf of the king

2:7 I will tell of the decree of the LORD:
    He said to me, "You are my son;
    today I have begotten you.
2:8 Ask of me, and I will make the nations
      your heritage,
    and the ends of the earth your possession.
2:9 You shall break them with a rod of iron,
    and dash them in pieces like a potter's vessel."
	Content of the oracle: God's institution of the new king and promise of support

2:10 Now therefore, O kings, be wise;
    be warned, O rulers of the earth.
2:11 Serve the LORD with fear, with trembling
2:12 kiss his feet,
    or he will be angry, and you will perish in
      the way;
    for his wrath is quickly kindled.
	Exhortation to submission

Happy are all who take refuge in him.	Conclusion: blessing

LITERARY GENRE AND HISTORICAL CONTEXT

Psalm 2 was most probably composed on occasion of the enthronement[44] of the new Davidic king, the time when vassal kings would attempt to revolt. The psalm can be contemplating either a historic or an idealistic situation.[45] In any case, it affirms that God guarantees the perpetuation of the dynasty. Dahood dates it from the tenth century BC because of its archaic language,[46] Mowinckel also as preexilic, and A. Robert as postexilic, but his argument is weak.

A good complement of Ps 2 is Ps 72, which describes the virtues of the ideal king. The fact that different persons speak in the psalm (the psalmist in vv. 1–2; the pagan nations in v. 3; the psalmist in vv. 4–5; God in v. 6; the king in vv. 7–9; the psalmist or the king in vv. 10–12), makes it plausible to think that the psalm was spoken by different people in the liturgy of coronation:

The priests: vv. 1–6
The king: vv. 7–9
The congregation: vv. 10–12

This royal psalm, applied to the new descendant of David who would sit on the throne, acquired an eschatological and messianic connotation after the exile (according to Craigie, Podechard, etc.),[47] idealizing the virtues and power of the future anointed king. But for Castellino,[48] the psalm indeed had a messianic connotation already at the time of the monarchy: the people would expect that with the new king, there would be the fulfillment of the promise made to David.

NOTES

> vv. 1–3 The issue of a coalition of different kings against another king was not unusual: for example, the coalition of the king of Aram and the king of Israel against the king of Judah (Isa 7:1).[49] But in the case of the revolt alluded to in Ps 2, and described as "vain," the situation of submission is broken (v. 3) at the time when there is a gap between the death of a king and the coronation of a new one. The word *anointed* (v. 2) is designated by the Hebrew word משיח, *māshîaḥ* ("messiah"), and rendered into Greek by the word Χριστός, *christos* ("Christ"). The royal title of messiah derives from the fact that the king was anointed on his coronation (cf. 1 Kgs 1:45; 2 Kgs 11:12). The anointing symbolized the fact that the person had been chosen by God to lead and save his people (cf. 1 Sam 9:16b).
> vv. 4–6 The election of the king is linked to the election of Zion (v. 6), where God resides among his people.
> v. 7 Here we have an evocation of the promise made to David (2 Sam 7:14).[50] The adoption of the king as son by God fulfills the main idea of the covenant: to establish a union between God and his people (cf. Exod 6:7 "I will take you as my people, and I will be your God"). This goal is later

accomplished between God and the king, who represents the whole people (2 Sam 7:14 "I will be a father to him, and he shall be a son to me"). Divine adoption was a rite of the ancient Near East (in Egypt and Assyro-Babylon the king was considered son of a god); but the Israelite king was not divinized; hence, one has to understand the phrase "I have begotten you" as a poetical hyperbole. The mention of "today" meant that God's decree had become effective.

v. 9 The image of breaking in pieces a pottery vessel recalls the execration texts of the ancient Near East: the names of the enemies were written on ceramic pieces that were then shattered in order to symbolize their defeat.[51]

vv. 10–12 The role of the Israelite king reflects somehow the universal dominion of God over all nations (v. 11). Not to show submission to God will imply destruction (v. 12a), but submission will bring happiness (v. 12c).

v. 12 The conclusion with a beatitude parallels the beginning of Ps 1. It may have been added later to present Pss 1—2 as a unit, and as an introduction to the Psalter: the fidelity to the covenant (Ps 1:2) and trust in God and his messiah (2:6–9) synthesize roughly the theology of the Psalter. Psalms 1—2 present the main characters of the Psalter: the righteous and the impious, the nations and the Messiah of Israel.

CHRISTIAN APPROPRIATION

With Christ, this psalm has found its full meaning. Psalm 2 has been applied to Christ since the beginning of Christian preaching (cf. Acts 4:25–26; 13:33). It has been understood in the light of the messianic promise made to David (2 Sam 7:12, 14; see Acts 2:31–32; 3:26). The NT quotations underline, above all, the divine sonship of Christ (Ps 2:7) and his victory over the enemy (Ps 2:1–2, 8–9). This messianic psalm, then, offers motifs for a deep understanding of Christ; it is a christological meditation.

In particular, NT authors have related Psalm 2 to different moments of the life of Jesus:

Categories of Psalms

Verses 1–2 have been used to describe the arrest and condemnation of Jesus (Acts 4:25b–26).

Verse 7 has been related to a) his baptism (Luke 3:22b; cf. Matt 3:17b; Mark 1:11b), b) his transfiguration (cf. Matt 17:5b; Mark 9:7b; Luke 9:35b), c) his resurrection (Acts 13:33), and d) his ascension and glorification (Heb 1:5; 5:5).

Verse 8 is used in regard to the glorification of Christ (Heb 1:2).

Verse 9 is applied to the salvific work of Christ (Rev 12:5b).

It is notable, however, that while Ps 2 breathes an atmosphere of violence (cf. v. 9), the victory of Jesus was realized through his resurrection, and this distinguishes Jesus from any other human king.[52] This point is emphasized by Hebrews 1:5. Another difference is that Ps 2:8 presents a universal dominion, but Christ's dominion over all the earth still awaits its fulfillment. This is why the Book of Revelation quotes Ps 2 to describe the ultimate rule and triumph of Christ at the end of time (Rev 1:5; 2:27; 4:2; 6:17; 12:5; 19:5; etc.).[53]

This psalm offers a clear answer to the question, who rules over the world? The pagan nations or God? It is God through his messiah, even if at times, it does not seem so. The final invitation of the psalm is relevant in this context: "Happy are all who take refuge in him [God]" (Ps 2:12c). This is, in fact, the main idea of the supplication psalms that dominate the first half of the Psalter.

9. PSALMS OF THE FIDELITY OF YAHWEH

The *Sitz im Leben* of these psalms is probably a liturgy of the community and of the nation celebrating the fidelity of Yahweh. These feasts have their basis in the Deuteronomic tradition.[54] Such liturgies or feasts could have been celebrated according to what is prescribed in Deuteronomy 6:17–25.[55] However, it is not always clear whether these psalms were composed for a communal liturgy. For example, Ps 78 constitutes a long account of the events of the history of Israel, but it does not contain any explicit invitation to the people to praise God. Therefore, we can say that the most distinctive characteristic of these psalms is the evocation of the salvific actions of God on behalf of his people (cf. Deut 6:21–23; Josh 24:2–13). This retelling of what God has done should move the people to praise God and exhort the people to renew his fidelity to the covenant.

Hence, some characteristic elements of these psalms are the following:[56]

1. *Invitation to praise God with joy* (Pss 81:2–4; 95:1–2, 6; 105:1–2; 106:1–2)
2. *Reference to the commandments* (Pss 81:5–6; 78:5–6; 105:8–10)
3. *Discourse of the wonders of God in favor of his people* (Ps 105:12–25): mainly the wonders of the Exodus (Pss 81:7–8, 11; 105:26–44)
4. *Exhortation to be faithful to the covenant* (Pss 81:9–10; 95:8–11): this could also be done through the evocation of the infidelity of the people in the past (Pss 78; 81:12–13; 95:9–11) or the confession of the infidelity (Ps 106:6).

Concerning their appropriation, the psalms of the fidelity of Yahweh remind us that our faith in God is anchored in historical facts (history of salvation) and not in mere ideas (such as Greek philosophy or Gnosticism). It is a series of historical events that the people saw and had witnessed (cf. Ps 95:9, "They had seen my work"). But the recollection of past events is linked to one purpose: appeal to be faithful and thankful to God. In this sense, these psalms are similar to the psalms of supplication or thanksgiving. These psalms offer a theological view of history, since the enumeration or list of the historical events is always accompanied by praise to God.

We can classify under this category the following psalms: 78; 81; 95; 105; 106.

Categories of Psalms

EXAMPLE: PSALM 95

STRUCTURE

95:1 O come, let us sing to the LORD;
    let us make a joyful noise to the rock of
        our salvation!
95:2 Let us come into his presence with
        thanksgiving;
    let us make a joyful noise to him with
        songs of praise!
	Introduction: invitation to praise Yahweh

95:3 For the LORD is a great God,
    and a great King above all gods.
95:4 In his hand are the depths of the earth;
    the heights of the mountains are his also.
95:5 The sea is his, for he made it,
    and the dry land, which his hands have
        formed.
	Reason: the greatness of Yahweh

95:6 O come, let us worship and bow down, let us kneel before the LORD, our Maker!	Renewed invitation to praise Yahweh

95:7 For he is our God,
    and we are the people of his pasture,
    and the sheep of his hand.
	Reason: Yahweh's fidelity

O that today you would listen to his voice!
95:8 Do not harden your hearts, as at Meribah,
    as on the day at Massah in the wilderness,
95:9 when your ancestors tested me,
    and put me to the proof, though they
        had seen my work.
95:10 For forty years I loathed that generation
    and said, "They are a people whose hearts
        go astray,
    and they do not regard my ways."
95:11 Therefore in my anger I swore,
    "They shall not enter my rest."
	Exhortation to be faithful by evoking the infidelity of the people in the past

LITERARY GENRE

This psalm appears as a hymn to be sung at the introductory procession to the temple (v. 2a)—that is the reason for being used at the beginning of the liturgical office. One can distinguish two major parts: praise and commemoration (vv. 1-7b), and an admonition (vv. 7c-11).

But what chiefly characterizes this psalm is the contrast between the greatness of God, who is faithful to his people (vv. 1, 7), and the infidelity of the people (vv. 8-10), while it also recalls some of the events of the wandering in the desert (Meribah and Massah, vv. 8-10). This leads us to classify this psalm as a psalm of the fidelity of Yahweh.

Some scholars (e.g., Olhausen, Buttenweiser, and Briggs), have suggested distinguishing two separate psalms: a hymn of praise (95:1-7c) and a divine oracle (95:7d-11); but most scholars (Gunkel, Mowinckel, Castellino) maintain the literary unity of the psalm. Others have emphasized the admonitory part as the dominant characteristic of the psalm, and consequently classify this psalm as a prophetic exhortation (Sabourin).[57] However, Westermann[58] and Gerstenberger have compared these prophetic speeches (mostly found in the Books of Chronicles) with the original forms of the prophetic judgment speech and found that the preaching in Pss 50, 81, and 95 has lost some of the immediacy of earlier prophetic oracles. Rather, these forms of prophetic preaching were most at home in circles of Levitical priests in the exilic and postexilic periods.[59]

HISTORICAL CONTEXT

Identifying the historical context of this psalm is not easy. Among those who maintain the unity of the psalm, Leslie has proposed to see in the first part of the psalm (vv. 1-7c) the invitation to come to praise God, and in the second part (vv. 7d-11) the intervention of a cultic prophet or a priest with a prophetic spirit who speaks an oracle warning the entire worship crowd against breaking the covenant (e.g., Amos in Bethel: Amos 7:10-13). The historical setting would be then a liturgical celebration related to the renewal of the covenant.

This feast would appear to have been celebrated in the spirit of the Deuteronomic tradition. In fact, the abrupt shift in this psalm already appears in the Deuteronomic discourses, where the exhortation to remain faithful to the covenant (Deut 8:1–6) was accompanied by a strong warning not to transgress the law of the Lord (Deut 8:11–20). And in particular, the revolt at Meribah and Massah is mentioned several times in the Book of Deuteronomy (Meribah in Deut 32:51 and Massah in Deut 6:16; 9:22; 33:8).

But the identification of the exact feast in which the psalm was used is still debated. It may have been at the celebration of the enthronement of Yahweh as King (cf. v. 3) during the civil new year festival (the first day of the seventh month, Tishri),[60] where the first part of the psalm would mark the epiphany or theophany of God, and the second part would mark the renewal of the covenant (Mowinckel). On the other hand, it may have been at the Feast of the Tabernacles[61] (see Ps 81:1, 9–17; Deut 31:10–13) (Sabourin); in fact, there are several examples of prophet-priests preaching in the middle of those feasts (Deut 27:9–10; 31:9–13).

While the language of the psalm suggests an ancient date of composition[62] (cf. v. 3b), the psalm continued to be used after the exile. In fact, in the Jewish tradition, Ps 85 was used in evening worship in the synagogues at the beginning of the Sabbath and also as invitatory psalm in worship services.[63]

NOTES

One can distinguish two major parts to this psalm: a praise (95:1–7c) and an admonition (95:7d–11).

v. 1 The invitation, "O come, let us…" is repeated three times in the first part of the psalm. Some scholars (Oesterley, Leslie) have seen three progressive stages: the first invitation (v. 1) happens when they approach the sanctuary, the second invitation envisions worshipers about to enter into the inner court of the temple, and the third invitation calls on the worshipers to enter further into the inner place and bow down before Yahweh.[64] But it is also possible to consider that the three invitations were only intended to be sung as a refrain by the entire congregation.[65]

v. 2 The metaphor of the rock can allude to the rock at Meribah (cf. v. 8) from which came out water (Exod 17:6).

v. 3 The affirmation of practical monotheism (only God acts over other gods) betrays the antiquity of the psalm, from a time when polytheism still existed.

v. 4 The proclamation of God's power over creation as a basis for obeying the commandments is also a motif mentioned in the Deuteronomic tradition (Deut 10:12–14). Kraus[66] has noticed that God is presented as creator of the world in verses 3–5 and as creator of Israel in verses 6–7.

vv. 7c–11 There is an admonition to the people based on Exodus 17:7: do not be unfaithful to God! The people are already in the promised land and seem to enjoy the repose; the danger is in thinking that they have reached their final goal and thus forgetting their responsibility toward the covenant.

v. 7d The people have to keep the covenant "today" (v. 7c). The emphasis on "today" is characteristic of Deuteronomy (Deut 4:40; 5:3; 6:6; 7:11). The mention of "today" serves to link the past events that are about to be mentioned (vv. 8–10) with the present.

v. 9 The motif of the "testing" ("Massah")[67] of God is also present in the Deuteronomic tradition (Deut 6:16; 33:8).

v. 11 If the people do not obey the covenant, they will behave like the people who revolted in the desert and will not enter into the "rest" of God (v. 11). While the concept of "rest" in the Deuteronomic history refers only to the promised land (Deut 12:9; Josh 1:13), in the postexilic period it came, rather, to symbolize a spiritual place: the place where God resides (2 Chr 6:41; Ps 95:11). According to Tate,[68] Hebrews 3:7—4:11 (especially 4:11) is a Christian midrash on Ps 95.

CHRISTIAN APPROPRIATION

Psalm 95 stands out for giving more space to the praise of God than to the recording of the salvific acts of God. This psalm helps us to meditate on the decision to be made between fidelity or infidelity, a decision that has to be made "today" (v. 7b). This psalm also reminds us that worship is more than simply remembering the past deeds of God on behalf of his people, but is a present ("today" v. 7d) call to obey God. The praise to God (vv. 1–2, 6) has to be accompanied by obedience to God (vv. 7d–8).

The author of the Letter to the Hebrews quotes this psalm (Heb 3:7–11) to exhort the believers to be faithful: they form part of the history of salvation (cf. Heb 11) and have to do their part to collaborate to the establishment of the kingdom of God.

The liturgy of the church uses this psalm as an invitatory psalm that opens the daily divine office.

10. WISDOM PSALMS

Some psalms reveal a wisdom style and vocabulary: for example, the use of the proverb form, and the presentation of the theme of retribution. These criteria suggest that the following psalms should be classified as wisdom psalms: 1; 9; 10; 12; 14; 15; 36; 37; 49; 52; 53; 73; 91; 94; 112; 119; 127; 128; 139.

These psalms do not present a definitive structure.[69] Their *Sitz im Leben* could be seen in the atmosphere of the wisdom teaching, but we cannot be more precise than that.

The wisdom tradition in Israel was a practical teaching in how to live well and to achieve happiness, what we could call "philosophy about life." The classical teaching was be good and avoid sin. But such a principle seemed to be wrong, since one could see the sinner becoming rich and powerful, and the just oppressed and suffering. Wisdom literature faced this difficult issue and gave different answers: Qohelet seems to give a pessimistic answer; the Book of Job appears to expect resignation, but this still seems unsatisfactory. The wisdom psalms give their own answer (or four different answers):[70]

1. The first group of wisdom psalms simply does not consider the problem; instead, it affirms that we have to wait and see how the wicked are punished and the righteous

flourish. This group of psalms holds the classical principle: the righteous are blessed, sinners are punished (Pss 1; 15; 52; 112; 119; 127; 128).
2. The second group acknowledges the problem and asks God to reestablish the equilibrium: to punish the wicked and to reward the just (Pss [9]; 10; 12; 14; 94).
3. The third group goes one step further, denying the value of the prosperity of the wicked and stressing the true value of the righteous: the enjoyment of God and his approval (Pss 36; 91; 139).
4. The fourth group gives the ultimate answer of the OT to the problem: beyond the reality of this world, the psalmist hopes for a special kind of life and enjoyment of God; it does not confess clearly the belief in the afterlife, but it goes beyond the closed shadows of Sheol (Pss 17;[71] 37; 49; 73). In particular, Ps 37 presents the being with God and the reception "in glory" as the greatest good (Ps 37:4-6, 11, 18, 29, 34, 39), being sure of the ruin of the wicked (Ps 37:9a, 28b, 38).

This list, however, is compiled according to logical similarities, not according to a chronological order that could reveal the idea of a religious evolution of the idea of retribution.[72] In ancient Israel different traditions were alive simultaneously.

Concerning their appropriation, we have to say that the wisdom psalms offer a different view on life: they do not speak with the passionate language of the supplication psalms or thanksgiving psalms, but with a peaceful view on those values that are many times put to the test in life. They remind us of the perennial value and certainty of the religious values that give direction to our life. Some of them point to a deep belief that goes beyond the common beliefs of the OT, foretelling the newness of the NT.

Categories of Psalms

EXAMPLE: PSALM 1

STRUCTURE

1:1 Happy are those
    who do not follow the advice of
        the wicked,
    or take the path that sinners tread,
    or sit in the seat of scoffers;
1:2 but their delight is in the law of
        the LORD,
    and on his law they meditate day
        and night.
1:3 They are like trees
    planted by streams of water,   *comparison*
    which yield their fruit in its season,
    and their leaves do not wither.
    In all that they do, they prosper.   *destiny*

[The way of the righteous]

1:4 The wicked are not so,
    but are like chaff that the wind   *comparison*
        drives away.
1:5 Therefore the wicked will not stand in   *destiny*
        the judgement,
    nor sinners in the congregation of
        the righteous;

[The way of the sinner]

1:6 for the LORD watches over the way of
        the righteous,
    but the way of the wicked will perish.

[Conclusion]

HISTORICAL CONTEXT

The theme of the two ways is characteristic of Deuteronomy (Deut 30:15–20) (ca. seventh century BC), but this similarity does not provide any clue for the date. The similarity of Ps 1:3 to Jeremiah 17:7–8 (ca. seventh century BC) has been interpreted in opposite ways: some consider that Ps 1 depends on Jeremiah 17 and therefore consider the psalm as postexilic, and others consider that Jeremiah 17 depends on Ps 1 (Kirkpatrick) and therefore regard the psalm as preexilic.

On the other hand, the emphasis on the law on which the pious Jew meditates (Ps 1:2) is characteristic of postexilic wisdom (Sir 24) and thus favors dating the psalm to the fifth to fourth century BC. Furthermore, the theme of "happiness" (v. 1) is typical of the wisdom tradition (Prov 3:13; 8:32, 34). Consequently, a postexilic date seems more reasonable.

LITERARY GENRE AND THEOLOGY

This psalm appears to be a didactic or educative poem that does not seem to have been composed for liturgical use but for personal meditation (Mowinckel) or as a literary setting as an introduction to the Psalter. In fact, according to the Talmud (*Ber.* 9b), Ps 1 and Ps 2 formed a unit and constitute an introduction to the Psalter. This view is also found in the early Christian tradition, since in Acts 13:33, Ps 2:7 is quoted as if it were the first psalm.

While Pss 1 and 2 were most probably separate compositions, they seem to have been put together by the final redactor of the Psalter (notice the inclusion: Ps 1:1, "Happy are those…"; Ps 2:12, "Happy are they…").[73] Psalm 1 would be the wisdom or moral preface to the Psalter, and Ps 2 the prophetic preface (announcing the Messiah). It has also been suggested that Pss 1 and 2 were united to form a coronation liturgy in which the king pledged to keep the law.[74]

In particular, Ps 1 appears to be the introduction to the entire Psalter, presenting the "two ways": one that leads to blessing (vv. 1–3) and the other to destruction (vv. 4–5). It recalls the discourse of Moses to the people of Israel before entering the promised land (Deut 11:26–29; 30:15–20). The theme of the two ways that already appears in the OT wisdom tradition (cf. Prov 4:18–19) became prominent in apostolic literature (cf. *Didache* 1:1).

This psalm also presents the classical doctrine of retribution: the righteous are blessed by God and the wicked are punished (Prov 2:21–22; 4:18–19). What is clear in this psalm is that the way of the righteous and the way of the wicked are two different, irreconcilable ways.

The use of parallelism is abundant in the psalm (vv. 1, 2, 3c–d, 5, 6). The psalm begins with the first letter of the Hebrew alphabet א (*'ālef*): אשרי (*'ashrê* = "happy") and ends with the last letter ת (*taw*): תאבד (*tō'bēd* = "perish"): Ps 1 offers a complete instruction going from A to Z on the way of life.

NOTES

v. 1 The psalm opens with a blessing: "Happy are those…" The conclusion of the psalm indicates the main reason for this happiness: the Lord watches over their lives (v. 6).

vv. 1–3 The blessing is for the person who practices (v. 1) and meditates on (v. 2) the law. The eulogy or praise of the law (v. 3) was a main theme of the wisdom tradition (cf. Sir 24:23). The image of the tree by streams of water is meaningful in the arid Holy Land; it can also recall the messianic waters of Ezekiel 47:12.

v. 5 A question exists as to whether the judgment is the ongoing judgment by God or the final eschatological judgment. Since the psalter seems to have been finalized by the third to second century BC, we can suppose the judgment to be eschatological (cf. Mal 3:2). But it can comprise both judgments, where the final is only the completion of the continuous judgment. Instead of "will not stand," the Greek version uses the word αναστήσονται, *anastēsontai*, and the Latin uses *resurgent*, suggesting that this verse should be related to the final judgment and the resurrection.

CHRISTIAN APPROPRIATION

The universal language of Ps 1 allows us to apply it to all of humanity and to each particular individual in his or her responsibility before God. Through this psalm, we can pray for the whole world to learn the way of the righteous and not the way of sin. In Christ, we have the personification of the true "way" (cf. John 14:6, "I am the way") and of the word of God (cf. John 1:14, "And the Word became flesh"); Christ is the one who teaches the word of God. The Christian life is a pilgrimage following the way of Christ. In the Letter to the Hebrews, Christ is presented as the pioneer of our salvation (Heb 2:10; 12:2).

11. DIFFERENT PSALMS

A small group of five psalms belonging to the postexilic period constitutes a separate group. They present a simple structure, lacking the multiplicity of themes or parts as in the previous groups of psalms.

According to their simple theme, they could be classified under the other categories; but it is perhaps better to leave them apart. So Ps 121 presents the continuous and lovely divine protection; Ps 123 deals with the hope for the divine mercy; Ps 126 depicts the reality of the liberation; Ps 133 describes the beauty of love among brothers and sisters; and Ps 134 is an invitation to praise God day and night in his sanctuary.

EXAMPLE: PSALM 133

STRUCTURE

A Song of Ascents.

133:1 How very good and pleasant it is when kindred live together in unity!	Introduction: the blessing of unity
133:2 It is like the precious oil on the head, running down upon the beard, on the beard of Aaron, running down over the collar of his robes.	Comparison: like the fragrance of perfume
133:3 It is like the dew of Hermon, which falls on the mountains of Zion.	Comparison: like the freshness of the dew
For there the LORD ordained his blessing, life for evermore.	Conclusion: the Lord gives his blessing

NOTES

According to St. Augustine (PL 37, 1729), this psalm on fraternal concord has begotten monasteries. Scholars believe that this psalm was composed when the value of brotherhood was in danger.

Ps 133 appears to be a wisdom teaching on the beauty of brotherly unity. The added title suggests that it was probably used for the final stage of the ascent to the temple: when the people were gathered in the temple. Nowadays it is used in Israel in reference to the family.

v. 1 The introduction affirms the value of the unity of brothers and sisters.

v. 2 It has been suggested (by Kirkpatrick) that the psalm would date from the time of the restoration of the Jewish community by Nehemiah. Therefore, the search for unity would be encouraged and promoted by the priests (so the mention of Aaron in v. 2).

v. 3a The simile of the dew (Kirkpatrick) would symbolize the benefit of unity upon the whole nation, in the same way as the dew refreshes the vegetation.

v. 3b It is not clear whether the blessing of God is upon Zion (v. 3a) or upon the community. However, it can be said that the Jewish community is united only because of God.

CHRISTIAN APPROPRIATION

Psalm 133 is a praise of the community that can be applied to the liturgical gathering, the family, the community of friends, or the whole church. It reminds us that the unity is wanted by God and blessed with goodness and joy (cf. v. 1) and God wants it as "eternal life" (cf. v. 3).

The Psalms

NOTES

1. Most of what follows is taken from the works of BONORA and CASTELLINO: A. BONORA, "Salmi," in *Il Messaggio della Salvezza*, ed. F. Festorazzi, vol. 5 (Turin: Elle Di Ci, 1985), 193–205; G. CASTELLINO, *Libro dei Salmi*, La Sacra Bibbia (Roma-Torino: Marietti, 1955); S. MOWINCKEL, *The Psalms in Israel's Worship*, 2 vols. (London: Blackwell, 1962; repr., 1 vol., Grand Rapids: Eerdmans, 2004). Cf. also H. GUNKEL, *Introduction to Psalms: The Genres of the Religious Lyric of Israel* (Macon, GA: Mercer University Press, 1998). For an easy introduction, see J. D. PLEINS, *The Psalms: Songs of Tragedy, Hope and Justice* (Maryknoll, NY: Orbis, 1993).

2. GUNKEL prefers the term *lamentation* instead of *supplication*. However, *supplication* seems preferable since the lament (i.e., the evocation of the situation of distress) is not the dominant element. In fact, the psalmist recalls the past or the painful present not with resignation, but with the intent that God intervene. The supplication or petition for salvation is the dominant element. Richard CLIFFORD suggests using the term *petition* (CLIFFORD, *Psalms 1—72*, AOTC [Nashville: Abingdon, 2002], 21). On this kind of psalm, see Richard J. DILLON, "The Psalms of the Suffering Just," *Worship* 61 (1987): 430–40.

3. On the enemies in the psalms, see T. R. HOBBS and P. K. JACKSON, "The Enemy in the Psalms," *BTB* 21 (1991): 22–29; George W. ANDERSON, "Enemies and Evildoers in the Book of Psalms," *BJRL* 48 (1965–66): 18–29.

4. In order to understand correctly the imprecations, we have to take into account two things: 1) there is an exclusive choice between good and evil: one cannot serve both; therefore what is at stake is not vengeance but the desire of choosing good and consequently rejecting evil. 2) The psalmist ultimately appeals to God's righteousness; although the psalmist asks for the destruction of his or her enemies, he or she leaves his or her cause to God. Ultimately, the thirst for righteousness present in these imprecations is considered as a blessing (cf. Matt 5:6). The Catholic Church decided to remove the imprecatory verses from the liturgy out of regard for "the weak." But a real solution to this problem consists in a correct teaching of how to pray with those imprecatory sentences (cf. the article by L. ALONSO-SCHÖKEL in Aa.Vv., *Esegesi ed ermeneutica*, 249, Atti della XXI Settimana Biblica (Brescia: Paideia, 1972). See also Erich ZENGER, *A God of Vengeance: Understanding the Psalms of Divine Wrath* (Louisville, KY: Westminster John Knox Press, 1994); Johannes G. Vos, "The Ethical Problem of the Imprecating

Psalms," *WTJ* 4 (1992): 123-38; John L. McKenzie, "The Imprecations of the Psalter," *AER* 111 (1944): 81-96.

5. J. Becker, *Wege der Psalmenexegese*, SBS 78 (Stuttgart: KBW Verlag, 1975), 59-65.

6. E. Balla, *Das Ich der Psalmen* (Göttingen: Vandenhoeck and Ruprecht, 1912).

7. The classification varies between authors. The list provided here, taken mainly from Castellino, is intended only as an approximate guide.

8. Lorenzin, *I Salmi*, I Libri Biblici 20 (Milano: Paoline, 2001), 67.

9. P. E. Bonnard, *Le Psautier selon Jérémie*, LD 26 (Paris: Cerf, 1960).

10. J. Coppens, "Les Psaumes 6 et 41 dépendent-ils du livre de Jeremie?," *HUCA* 32 (1961): 217-26.

11. R. C. Culley, *Oral Formulaic Language in the Biblical Psalms* (Toronto: University of Toronto Press, 1967), 105.

12. This would be the counterpart of the victory hymn of Judg 5.

13. If we accept the identification of the reference to the first person singular "I" as the king, then the psalm could have originally been composed in the preexilic monarchy, when the king was commanding the army of Israel.

14. So P. Craigie, *Psalms 1-50*, WBC 19 (Waco, TX: Word Books, 1983), 332.

15. The Feast of Hanukkah (*b. Sop.* 18b). However, according to the Mishnah, the psalm was also used for the feast of the presentation of the first fruits (*Bik.*3:4; cf. Deut 26:1-11); quoted by Craigie, *Psalms 1-50*, 253.

16. For these notes, we follow Craigie, *Psalms 1-50*, 253-55.

17. The cohortative mode is a verb form that does not exist in English. It only appears in the first person plural; its closest translation would be "Let us."

18. So, for example, A. Anderson, *Psalms*, 2 vols, NCBC (Grand Rapids: Eerdmans), 1:100. The mention of "David" in the title of the psalm would reinforce this cultic usage.

19. So E. S. Gerstenberger, *Psalms*, part 1, FOTL 14 (Grand Rapids: Eerdmans, 1988), 70-72.

20. Craigie, *Psalms 1-50*, 109.

21. On the use of the "name" of God in this psalm, see R. Tournay, "Le Psaume VIII et la doctrine biblique du nom," *RB* 78 (1971): 18-30.

22. Craigie, *Psalms 1-50*, 110.

23. On the Psalms of Ascents, see Cuthbert C. Keet, *A Study of the Psalms of Ascents: A Critical and Exegetical commentary upon Psalms CXX to CXXXIV* (London: The Mitre Press, 1969).

24. L. ALLEN, *Psalms 101—150*, WBC 21 (Waco TX: Word Books, 1983), 159.

25. Ibid., 157.

26. H. KRAUS, *Theologie der Psalmen* (Neukirchen-Vluyn: Neukirchener Verlag, 1979), 1017.

27. H. GUNKEL, *Die Psalmen*, HKAT (Göttingen: Vandenhoeck & Ruprecht, 1926, 1968), 543.

28. A. WEISER, *The Psalms: A Commentary*, trans. Herbert Hartwell, OTL (Philadelphia: Westminster Press, 1982), 750.

29. G. WANKE, *Die Zionstheologie der Korachiten in ihrem traditionsgeschichtlichen Zusammenhang*, BZAW 97 (Berlin: De Gruyter, 1966), 106-7.

30. L. SABOURIN, *The Psalms: Their Origin and Meaning* (New York: Alba House, 1974), 214.

31. The Hebrew word '*îr* (v.3), which means "city," repeats the sound of the first syllable of the word *yerûshalāim* (*yerû*), which means "Jerusalem"; and the Hebrew word *shalôm*, which means "peace," repeats the second part of the word *yerûshalāim* (-*shalāim*).

32. St. Jerome and St. Augustine interpreted this psalm in reference to the heavenly Jerusalem.

33. On the kingship of God, see John H. EATON, *Kingship and the Psalms*, 2nd ed., JSOT 35 (Sheffield: JSOT Press, 1986); J. D. W. WATTS, "Yahweh Malak Psalms," *TZ* 21 (1965), 341-48.

34. Several scholars, following GUNKEL, have proposed to see the feast of new year as the *Sitz im Leben* for these psalms on the kingship of Yahweh: P. VOLZ, *Das Neujahrfest Jahves*, SGV 67 (Tübingen: Mohr Siebeck, 1912); S. MOWINCKEL, *Psalmenstudien II: Das Thronbesteigungsfest Jahwäh's und der Ursprung der Eschatologie* (Kristiania: SNVAO, 1922), who spoke of the *Thronfart* or the *Thronbesteigung* ("ascension to the throne," "crowning"). However, this theory has been criticized: Laszlo J. PAPP, *Das Israelitische Neujahrfest* (Kampen: J. H. Kok, 1933); Moses BUTTENWEISER, *Psalms, Chronologically Treated with a New Translation*, The Library of Biblical Studies (Jersey City, NJ: KTAV Publishing House, 1969), 321-24; O. EISSFELDT, "Jahweh als König," *ZAW NF* 5 (1928): 81-105.

35. Jews used to celebrate the first day of the lunar month (New Moon, 2 Kgs 4:23); and the beginning of the seventh month was considered as the first day of the civil year (Lev 23:24; Num 29:1; note in the *New Jerusalem Bible* to Ps 81:4).

36. The NRSV translates the name of "Yahweh" with "the LORD"; instead, the NJB has kept the word "Yahweh."

37. It is to notice that the exaltation of the king and his kingdom was not exclusive of Israel. Rather, in the ancient Near East, the exaltation is exaggerated to the point of considering the king really as a divine being. In Israel the exaltation was only in the metaphorical sense, since the strict monotheism forbade considering the king as divine. Furthermore, in opposition to other nations where the king was divinized, in Israel it was the divinity that comes down to help and assist the human king.

38. H. CAZELLES, *Le Messie de la Bible* (Paris: Cerf, 1978). The prophets accomplished the conflation of the Davidic kingdom with the messianic kingdom.

39. The precise determination of these psalms is a debated question in biblical scholarship. See John I. DURHAM, "The King as 'Messiah' in the Psalms," *RevExp* 81 (1984): 425-35.

40. CRAIGIE, *Psalms 1-50*, 68-69.

41. CASTELLINO, *Salmi*, 590.

42. Corporate personality: the king stands for all the people.

43. LORENZIN notices that according to the Talmud, the rabbis discussed around AD 90 whether David had written the psalms for himself or for the community. They concluded that he wrote them in regard to himself and in regard to the whole community (*b. Pesaḥ* 114a; cf. *b. Ber.* 3a.) (LORENZIN, *Psalmi*, 32).

44. CRAIGIE classifies it more precisely as a coronation psalm (CRAIGIE, *Psalms 1—50*, 64).

45. CASTELLINO, *Salmi*, 590.

46. DAHOOD, *Psalms I*, 7.

47. E.g., CRAIGIE, *Psalms 1-50*, 68.

48. CASTELLINO, *Salmi*, 590.

49. There is a close parallel to Ps 2:1-2 in the oracles on Assurbanipal (PRITCHARD, *ANET*, 451, lines 8-13).

50. This promise is mentioned in several texts of the OT: 1 Chr 17:10-14; Pss 89:20-30; 132:11, 17-18.

51. K. SEYBOLD, *Die Psalmen*, HAT 1/15 (Tübingen: Mohr-Siebeck, 1996), 32-33.

52. CRAIGIE, *Psalms 1-50*, 69.

53. Ibid.

54. In fact, W. HARRINGTON proposes to call these psalms Psalms of a Deuteronomical Liturgy (HARRINGTON, *Record of the Promise: The Old Testament* [Chicago: The Priory Press, 1965], 311).

55. On this liturgy, cf. CASTELLINO, *Salmi*, 677-81.

56. Not necessarily all these characteristics are present in these psalms; Ps 81 displays all of them.

The Psalms

57. Sabourin considers this section as the most important and hence classifies this psalm as a "prophetic exhortation" (Sabourin, *Psalms*, 394). Other "prophetic exhortations" according to Sabourin are Pss 14; 50; 52; 53; 75; 81; 95 (ibid., 395).

58. C. Westermann, *Basic Forms of Prophetic Speech* (Philadelphia: Westminster Press, 1967), 163–68.

59. Marvin E. Tate, *Psalms 51—100*, WBC 20 (Dallas, TX: Word Books, 1990), 503.

60. This was during the New Moon (dark moon) of the month of Tishri.

61. This feast was celebrated during the Full Moon of the seventh month: on the fifteenth day of Tishri.

62. The opinion of commentators concerning the date of the psalm's composition varies greatly: early premonarchical years (A. R. Johnson), preexilic (Mowinckel), early postexilic (Tate), later postexilic (Gunkel, Oesterley).

63. Tate, *Psalms 51—100*, 499.

64. Ibid., 498, 501.

65. Ibid., 501.

66. Kraus, *Psalms*, 2:831.

67. For "Massah" (מסה, with the meaning of "trial" or "temptation,") see Deut 4:34; 7:19; 29:2.

68. Tate, *Psalms 51—100*, 498, 503.

69. L. Sabourin, "Un classement littéraire des psaumes." *Sciences Ecclésiastiques* 16 (1964): 51–53. See also James L. Crenshaw, "Wisdom Psalms?" *CRBS* 8 (2000): 9–17; Roland Murphy, *Wisdom Literature and Psalms* (Abingdon: Abingdon Press, 1983); J. K. Kuntz, "The Canonical Wisdom Psalms of Ancient Israel: Their Rhetorical, Thematic, and Formal Dimensions," in *Rhetorical Criticism: Essays in Honor of James Muilenburg*, ed. J. J. Jackson and M. Kessler, PTMS 1 (Pittsburgh: Pickwick, 1974), 186–222.

70. Castellino, *Salmi*, 730–31; Harrington, *Promise*, 309–10.

71. Ps 17 is classified here as a wisdom psalm because of the theme, but according to its literary genre, it would belong to the group of individual supplications.

72. The Book of Job gives a more developed answer on the problem of retribution than that of Qohelet, although Qohelet was written after Job.

73. See also Acts 13:33 in the Western reading, which quotes Ps 2 but calls it Ps 1.

74. W. H. Brownlee, "Ps 1-2 as a Coronation Liturgy," *Bib* 52 (1971): 321–36.

OVERVIEW OF PSALM CLASSIFICATIONS*

Individual Supplications: 5; 6; 7; 13; 17; 22; 25; 26; 27:7-14; 28; 31; 35; 38; 39; 42/43; 51; 54—57; 59; 61; 63; 64; 69; 70 (= 40:14-18); 71; 86; 88; 102; 109; 120; 130; 140; 141—143.

Confidence Psalms: 3; 11; 16; 23; 27:1-6; 41; 62; 131.

Public Supplications: 44; 58; 60:7-14 (= 108); 74; 77; 79; 80; 82; 83; 125.

Thanksgiving Psalms:
    a) Private: 4; 18; 30; 32; 34; 40:2-11; 66; 92; 116; 118; 138.
    b) Public: 124; 129.

Hymns: 8; 19; 29; 33; 65; 67; 68; 85; 100; 103; 104; 111; 113; 114; 117; 135; 136; 145—150.

Zion Psalms: 24; 46; 48; 76; 84; 87; 122; 137.

"Yahweh is King" Psalms: 47; 75; 93; 96—99.

Royal (Messianic) Psalms: 2; 20; 21; 45; 72; 89; 101; 110; 132; 144.

Psalms of the Fidelity of Yahweh: 50; 78; 81; 95; 105; 106; 115.

Wisdom Psalms: 1; 9; 10; 12; 14; 15; 36; 37; 49; 52; 53; 73; 91; 94; 112; 119; 127; 128; 139.

Different Prayers: 121; 123; 126; 133; 134

---

*This classification is taken from: G. CASTELLINO, *Libro dei Salmi*, La Sacra Bibbia (Roma-Torino: Marietti, 1955), ix–x.

THE PSALMS WITH THEIR PROPOSED LITERARY GENRES

1   Wisdom Psalm
2   Royal Psalm
3   Confidence Psalm
4   Private Thanksgiving Psalm
5   Individual Supplication
6   Individual Supplication
7   Individual Supplication
8   Hymn
9   Wisdom Psalm
10 (9)   Wisdom Psalm
11 (10)   Confidence Psalm
12 (11)   Wisdom Psalm
13 (12)   Individual Supplication
14 (13)   Wisdom Psalm
15 (14)   Wisdom Psalm
16 (15)   Confidence Psalm
17 (16)   Individual Supplication
18 (17)   Private Thanksgiving Psalm
19 (18)   Hymn
20 (19)   Royal Psalm
21 (20)   Royal Psalm
22 (21)   Individual Supplication
23 (22)   Confidence Psalm
24 (23)   Zion Psalm
25 (24)   Individual Supplication
26 (25)   Individual Supplication
27 (26)   Individual Supplication
28 (27)   Individual Supplication
29 (28)   Hymn
30 (29)   Private Thanksgiving Psalm

The Psalms

31 (30)	Individual Supplication
32 (31)	Private Thanksgiving Psalm
33 (32)	Hymn
34 (33)	Private Thanksgiving Psalm
35 (34)	Individual Supplication
36 (35)	Wisdom Psalm
37 (36)	Wisdom Psalm
38 (37)	Individual Supplication
39 (38)	Individual Supplication
40 (39)	Private Thanksgiving Psalm
41 (40)	Confidence Psalm
42 (41)	Individual Supplication
43 (42)	Individual Supplication
44 (43)	Public Supplication
45 (44)	Royal Psalm
46 (45)	Zion Psalm
47 (46)	"Yahweh is King" Psalm
48 (47)	Zion Psalm
49 (48)	Wisdom Psalm
50 (49)	Psalm of the Fidelity of Yahweh
51 (50)	Individual Supplication
52 (51)	Wisdom Psalm
53 (52)	Wisdom Psalm
54 (53)	Individual Supplication
55 (54)	Individual Supplication
56 (55)	Individual Supplication
57 (56)	Individual Supplication
58 (57)	Public Supplication
59 (58)	Individual Supplication
60 (59)	Public Supplication
61 (60)	Individual Supplication
62 (61)	Confidence Psalm
63 (62)	Individual Supplication
64 (63)	Individual Supplication
65 (64)	Hymn
66 (65)	Private Thanksgiving Psalm
67 (66)	Hymn
68 (67)	Hymn

The Psalms with Their Proposed Literary Genres

69 (68)	Individual Supplication
70 (69)	Individual Supplication
71 (70)	Individual Supplication
72 (71)	Royal Psalm
73 (72)	Wisdom Psalm
74 (73)	Public Supplication
75 (74)	"Yahweh is King" Psalm
76 (75)	Zion Psalm
77 (76)	Public Supplication
78 (77)	Psalm of the Fidelity of Yahweh
79 (78)	Public Supplication
80 (79)	Public Supplication
81 (80)	Psalm of the Fidelity of Yahweh
82 (81)	Public Supplication
83 (82)	Public Supplication
84 (83)	Zion Psalm
85 (84)	Hymn
86 (85)	Individual Supplication
87 (86)	Zion Psalm
88 (87)	Individual Supplication
89 (88)	Royal Psalm
90 (89)	Public Supplication
91 (90)	Wisdom Psalm
92 (91)	Private Thanksgiving Psalm
93 (92)	"Yahweh is King" Psalm
94 (93)	Wisdom Psalm
95 (94)	Psalm of the Fidelity of Yahweh
96 (95)	"Yahweh is King" Psalm
97 (96)	"Yahweh is King" Psalm
98 (97)	"Yahweh is King" Psalm
99 (98)	"Yahweh is King" Psalm
100 (99)	Hymn
101 (100)	Royal Psalm
102 (101)	Individual Supplication
103 (102)	Hymn
104 (103)	Hymn
105 (104)	Psalm of the Fidelity of Yahweh
106 (105)	Psalm of the Fidelity of Yahweh

The Psalms

107 (106)	Private Thanksgiving Psalm
108 (107)	Public Supplication
109 (108)	Individual Supplication
110 (109)	Royal Psalm
111 (110)	Hymn
112 (111)	Wisdom Psalm
113 (112)	Hymn
114 (113)	Hymn
115 (113)	Psalm of the Fidelity of Yahweh
116 (114–5)	Private Thanksgiving Psalm
117 (116)	Hymn
118 (117)	Private Thanksgiving Psalm
119 (118)	Wisdom Psalm
120 (119)	Individual Supplication
121 (120)	Different Prayer
122 (121)	Zion Psalm
123 (122)	Different Prayer
124 (123)	Public Thanksgiving Psalm
125 (124)	Public Supplication
126 (125)	Different Prayer
127 (126)	Wisdom Psalm
128 (127)	Wisdom Psalm
129 (128)	Public Thanksgiving Psalm
130 (129)	Individual Supplication
131 (130)	Confidence Psalm
132 (131)	Royal Psalm
133 (132)	Different Prayer
134 (133)	Different Prayer
135 (134)	Hymn
136 (135)	Hymn
137 (136)	Zion Psalm
138 (137)	Private Thanksgiving Psalm
139 (138)	Wisdom Psalm
140 (139)	Individual Supplication
141 (140)	Individual Supplication
142 (141)	Individual Supplication
143 (1423)	Individual Supplication
144 (143)	Royal Psalm

The Psalms with Their Proposed Literary Genres

145 (144)	Hymn
146 (145)	Hymn
147 (146–7)	Hymn
148	Hymn
149	Hymn
150	Hymn

SELECT BIBLIOGRAPHY

GENERAL WORKS ON THE PSALMS

Alonso-Schökel, Luis. *A Manual of Hebrew Poetics*. SB 11. Rome: Biblical Institute Press, 2000.

Anderson, B. W. *Out of the Depths: The Psalms Speak for Us Today*. 3rd ed. Louisville: Westminster John Knox Press, 2000.

Bellinger, W. H. *Psalms. A Guide to Studying the Psalter*. 2nd ed. Grand Rapids: Eerdmans, 2012.

Bonora, A. "I Salmi." In *Il Messaggio della Salvezza*, edited by F. Festorazzi, 5:183–230. Turin: Elle Di Ci, 1985.

Brueggemann, Walter. *Praying the Psalms: Engaging Scripture and the Life of the Spirit*. 2nd ed. Eugene, OR: Wipf and Stock Publishers, 2007.

Crenshaw, James L. *The Psalms: An Introduction*. Grand Rapids: Eerdmans, 2001.

De Claissé-Walford, Nancy L. *Introduction to the Psalms: A Song from Ancient Israel*. Atlanta: Chalice Press, 2004.

Drijvers, Pius. *The Psalms: Their Structure and Meaning*. New York: Herder & Herder, 1965.

Eaton, J. H. *Kingship and the Psalms*. London: SCM Press, 1976.

Firth, David and Johnston, Philip, eds. *Interpreting the Psalms: Issues and Approaches*. Downers Grove, IL: InterVarsity Press Academic, 2005.

Futato, Mark D. *Interpreting the Psalms: An Exegetical Handbook*. Grand Rapids: Kregel Publications, 2007.

Gillingham, Susan, ed. *Jewish and Christian Approaches to the Psalms: Conflict and Convergence*. Oxford: Oxford University Press, 2013.

———. *Psalms through the Centuries*. Vol. 1. Oxford: Wiley-Blackwell, 2008.

Gunkel, Hermann. *The Psalms: A Form-Critical Introduction*. Translated by Thomas M. Horner. Biblical Series 19. Philadelphia: Fortress Press, 1967.

———. and Joachim Begrich. *Introduction to the Psalms: The Genres of the Religious Lyric of Israel.* Translated by James D. Nogalski. Macon, GA: Mercer University Press, 1998.

GUTHRIE, Harvey H. *Israel's Sacred Songs: A Study of Dominant Themes.* New York: Seabury Press, 1966.

HOLLADAY, W. L. *The Psalms through Three Thousand Years: Prayerbook of a Cloud of Witnesses.* Minneapolis, MN: Fortress Press, 1993.

HUNTER, Alastair G. *An Introduction to the Psalms.* New York: T & T Clark, 2008.

JACQUET, Louis. *Les Psaumes et le cœur de l'Homme. Etude textuelle, littéraire et doctrinale.* 3 vols. Gembloux: Duculot, 1975.

KRAUS, Hans-Joachim. *Theology of the Psalms.* Translated by Keith Crim. Continental Commentaries. Minneapolis: Fortress Press, 1992.

LAMB, J. A. *The Psalms in Christian Worship.* London: The Faith Press, 1962.

LEWIS, C. S. *Reflections on the Psalms.* San Diego: Harcourt Brace Jovanovich Publishers, 1958.

LONGMAN, Tremper III. *How to Read the Psalms.* Downers Grove: InterVarsity Press, 1988.

MAYS, James Luther. *The Lord Reigns: A Theological Handbook to the Psalms.* Louisville: Westminster John Knox Press, 1994.

McCANN, J. Clinton. *A Theological Introduction to the Book of Psalms: The Psalms as Torah.* Nashville: Abingdon Press, 1993.

MILLER, P. D. *Interpreting the Psalms.* Philadelphia: Fortress Press, 1986.

MOWINCKEL, Sigmund. *The Psalms in Israel's Worship.* Grand Rapids: Eerdmans, 2004.

MURPHY, Roland E. *The Gift of the Psalms.* Peabody, MA: Hendrickson, 2000.

PLEINS, J. David. *The Psalms: Songs of Tragedy, Hope and Justice.* Maryknoll, NY: Orbis Books, 1993.

PRÉVOST, Jean-Pierre. *A Short Dictionary of the Psalms.* Collegeville, MN: Liturgical Press, 1997.

SABOURIN, Leopold. *The Psalms: Their Origin and Meaning.* New York: Alba House, 1974.

Select Bibliography

SEYBOLD, Klaus. *Introducing the Psalms*. Edinburgh: T & T Clark, 1990.

STUHLMUELLER, Carroll. *The Spirituality of the Psalms*. Collegeville, MN: Liturgical Press, 2002.

WHYBRAY, Norman. *Reading the Psalms as a Book*. JSOTSS 222. Sheffield: Sheffield Academic Press, 1996.

WILSON, Gerald H. *The Editing of the Hebrew Psalter*. SBLDS 76. Chico, CA: Scholars Press, 1985; 2004.

MODERN COMMENTARIES

ALLEN, Leslie C. *Psalms 101—150*. WBC 21. Waco, TX: Word Books, 1983.

ANDERSON, A. A. *Psalms*. 2 vols. NCBC. Grand Rapids: Eerdmans, 1972.

BRUEGGEMANN, Walter. *The Message of the Psalms: A Theological Commentary*. Minneapolis: Augsburg Pub. House, 1984.

CARNITI, Cecilia and Luis ALONSO-SCHÖKEL. *Salmos*. Navarra: Verbo Divino, 1992.

CASTELLINO, G. *Libro dei Salmi*. La Sacra Bibbia. Roma-Torino: Marietti, 1955.

CLIFFORD, Richard J. *Psalms*. 2 vols. AOTC. Nashville, TN: Abingdon Press, 2002–3.

CRAIGE, Peter C. *Psalms 1—50*. WBC 19. Waco, TX: Word Books, 1983.

DAHOOD, Michael. *Psalms*. 3 vols. AB 16-17A. Garden City, NY: Doubleday, 1966-70.

DAVIDSON, Robert. *The Vitality of Worship: A Commentary on the Book of Psalms*. Grand Rapids: Eerdmans, 1998.

GERSTENBERGER, Erhard S. *Psalms. Part I*. FOTL 14. Grand Rapids: Eerdmans, 1988.

HOSSFELD, Frank Lothar and Erick ZENGER. *Psalms 2*. Hermeneia. Minneapolis: Fortress Press, 2005. This volume covers Pss 51—100.

———. *Psalms 3*. Hermeneia. Minneapolis: Fortress Press, 2011. This volume covers Pss 101—150.

KALT, Edmund. *Herder's Commentary on the Psalms*. Westminster, MD: Newman Press, 1961.

KIDNER, Derek. *Psalms 1—72*. TOTC. London: InterVarsity Press, 1973.

———. *Psalms 73—150*. TOTC. London: InterVarsity Press, 1973.

KRAUS, Hans-Joachim. *Psalms 1—59: A Commentary*. Minneapolis: Fortress Press, 1988.

———. *Psalms 60—150: A Commentary*. Minneapolis: Fortress Press, 1988.

LORENZIN, Tiziano. *I Salmi*. I Libri Biblici 20. Milano: Paoline, 2001.

RAVASI, Gianfranco. *Il Libro dei Salmi. Commento e attualizzazione*. 3 vols. Bologna: Edizioni Dehoniane, 1986.

TATE, Marvin E. *Psalms 51—100*. WBC 20. Dallas, TX: Word Books, 1990.

TERRIEN, Samuel. *The Psalms: Strophic Structure and Theological Commentary*. Critical Eerdmans Commentary. Grand Rapids: Eerdmans, 2003.

VANGEMEREN, Willem A. *Psalms*. The Expositor's Bible Commentary 5. Grand Rapids: Zondervan, 2008.

WEISER, Artur. *The Psalms: A Commentary*. Translated by Herbert Hartwell. OTL. Philadelphia: Westminster Press, 1982.